HELPING WOMEN
IN CRISIS

Other Books by Kay Marshall Strom

Chosen Families

John Newton: The Angry Sailor

*A Question of Submission: A Painful
Look at Wife Battering*

Special Women in the Bible

Helping Women in Crisis

A Handbook for People Helpers

KAY MARSHALL STROM

Ministry Resources Library

Zondervan Publishing House • Grand Rapids, MI

Helping Women in Crisis
Copyright © 1986 by Kay Marshall Strom

Ministry Resources Library is an imprint of Zondervan Publishing House,
1415 Lake Drive, S.E., Grand Rapids, Michigan 49506.

Library of Congress Cataloging in Publication Data

Strom, Kay Marshall, 1943–
   Helping women in crisis.

   Includes bibliographies.
   1. Church work with women—Handbooks, manuals, etc. I. Title.
BV4445.S77   1986   253.5'088042   86-8560
ISBN 0-310-33641-4

Edited by James E. Ruark

Printed in the United States of America

86 87 88 89 90 91 92 / 10 9 8 7 6 5 4 3

CONTENTS

HELPING WOMEN
IN CRISIS

1. Who? Why? How?

"Be patient. God's not finished with me yet!"

"I'm not perfect, just forgiven!"

We see catchy slogans reminding us of our imperfections on bumper stickers, posters, buttons, pencils—even Frisbees. Unlikely places to find profound truth? To be sure! Yet profound truth it is. Jesus said it this way: "Let him who is without sin cast the first stone."

All of us, however religious and devout, are affected by sin, both our own and that of others. The results can be catastrophic. When faced with situations we cannot handle, we tend to reach out in desperation and grab hold of anyone we think may be able to help.

Counseling, especially in a time of crisis, is serious business. It is also an important and necessary ministry. If we are in a position where others look up to us as a spiritual leader—a minister or youth worker, perhaps, or a Bible study leader or Sunday school teacher, or maybe a Women's Ministries worker—it is very likely that eventually someone will turn to us for help, guidance, and advice.

Although it doesn't take an expert to be an effective people helper, not everyone can be one. Real helpers need to have certain Here-am-I-Lord-use-me characteristics. To find out if we have these traits we must ask ourselves the following questions:

- Do I have an honest concern for people who are hurting?
- Do I believe that God has the power to heal, however deep the hurt?
- Do I believe God can forgive, however great the sin?
- Am I willing to do whatever I can to help a hurting person?
- Am I willing to gain some basic knowledge of common crisis situations, of what to say and what not to say, of organizations and professionals to whom I can refer people for help?
- Can I recognize and accept my own limitations?

If we can answer yes to these questions, God can use us. Some Christians who are in excellent positions to provide real help to hurting people never do so because they do not believe that such awful things as wife abuse, child abuse and molestation, incest, alcoholism, and suicide happen within the Christian community. Are people who sit in church pews ever really involved in these things? Apparently so. Every one of these subjects has been the topic of one or more articles in recent issues of Christian magazines. And according to the response of their readerships, more than a few families are seeing in the horrors exposed a remarkable similarity to their own lives.

The fact that the Christian community is just now being awakened to these painful subjects does not mean that religious people are just now beginning to be affected by them. Rather, it would seem to indicate that subjects formerly considered unmentionable in Christian circles are finally being brought into the open. Though it may present us with some difficult counseling sessions, this situation is actually a good sign. Instead of being doomed to suffer in silence, victims and victimizers alike are finally beginning to come forward to ask for help, forgiveness, and healing.

Sin within the Christian community is not a new phenomenon. Indeed, the apostle Paul had a good deal to say about it. In Galatians 6:1 he told the church just what their response to such a situation should be: "Brothers, if someone is caught in a sin, you who are spiritual should restore him gently." Then he added this warning: "But watch yourself, or you also may be tempted" (NIV).

That's good advice. Not that all of us are in danger of falling into every sin we see in others. We aren't. The point is that we are all sinners, and we all have particular areas of vulnerability. If we can remember this, we will find it easier to love and accept a hurting person or family who comes to us regardless of what sin caused the problem. That is not to say that the sin should be condoned. Certainly not. The truth is that none of us is in a position to sit on a pedestal of self-righteousness and look down on someone who is entangled in sin. To do so would mean forgetting the forgiveness that the Lord has showered on us.

"The church was no help to me," a minister's wife commented bitterly. "When I turned to them, all I got were smooth-sounding platitudes. Their patronizing attitude was maddening and so frustrating!"

People who respond with simplistic answers to the pain of others undoubtedly mean well. The problem is that those nice-sounding phrases are much more comforting and encouraging to those who are saying them than they are to the people who are hurting. What the person in crisis needs is help—real, concrete, specific, down-to-earth help. That's what we should be prepared to give.

Fortunately many of the situations we encounter probably require little more than a listening ear, an attitude of loving concern, and a time of prayer together. When more is needed, we may be able to call on someone qualified to give extra help. The problem comes when we are presented with a crisis situation that demands immediate and aggressive action, and there is no one available but ourselves.

Some crises are life-threatening—a suicidal person, for instance, or a wife or child who is being beaten. Some situations are embarrassing. It's not pleasant to be told the details of an incestuous relationship or a horrifying rape or an adulterous affair.

During His lifetime Jesus was confronted by many people in unpleasant and socially unacceptable circumstances, yet He never turned them away. As Christians we are called to be Christ's representatives in this sinful and hurting world. When someone brings her problem to us, we have a responsibility to listen with loving, caring patience just as Christ Himself would have done.

Sometimes the person who comes to us will be a victim whose greatest need is to survive and, in time, to forgive. At other times she will see herself as the victim, but in listening to her story, we will feel certain that she is at least partly to blame. Our assessment may be right or it may be wrong. Then there will be times when the person who comes to us will clearly be guilty of the sin that has caused others great pain and suffering. Because of what she has done, she may also have hurt the cause of Christ. Regardless of where the fault lies, our position should be the same: God hates sin, but He loves sinners. No matter who is at fault, our attitude should remain one of helpful acceptance.

Because counselors, counselees, and individual situations vary so greatly, it is difficult to give specific rules for handling counseling situations. There are, however, some basic guidelines that we should always keep in mind when faced with a crisis:

Maintain Confidentiality—Usually

Confidentiality is a basic rule of counseling. What we are told in confidence must not be shared with anyone else without the approval of the person who confided in us. But in crisis counseling, this can

11

cause a dilemma. Suppose we are dealing with a situation involving serious abuse, the sexual molestation of a child, or perhaps a suicidal person. When someone is in physical danger, are we still bound by the rule of confidentiality? The answer is definitely No. In this instance you have a duty to report the situation to an appropriate social worker or public authority.

Look at All Sides

We must understand that the picture we get of what is happening may or may not be accurate. We are, after all, only hearing one side of what is surely a complex situation. Even if she is trying to be totally honest with us, the sufferer can only describe the matter from her own point of view. Is the woman really being beaten, as she says? Her husband may say that she is just angry and vengeful. Is her son really suicidal? He may say that she is overreacting. It is impossible for us to know for sure. To make things worse, appearances can be deceiving. A well-dressed, charming woman can indeed be an alcoholic. A "nice guy" can molest his daughter or beat his wife. Fortunately, though, diagnosis is not in our job description. For our purposes, we should assume in every case that the worst is true and proceed accordingly.

Take the Situation Seriously

Some situations may seem too incredible to be true, especially if we know any of the people involved. An alcoholic, for instance, can successfully hide her condition for years. So can an abused wife or an incestuous father. No matter how unbelievable it seems, it is vital that we take every situation seriously. A woman who comes to us concerned about her uncontrollable feelings toward her child should never be told, "Oh, everyone feels that way sometimes." What she feels may *not* be what everyone else feels. It is far better to err on the side of caution than to risk further harm or damage by ignoring the gravity of a problem.

Our Attitude

We cannot be effective counselors unless we are approachable, sensitive, and caring toward each person who comes to us for help. It is much easier to feel this way toward some people than others. A haughty person is more difficult than one who is contrite. A bitter person is more difficult to deal with than a tender one. Someone who has horribly victimized another is more difficult than the victim. The needy people will vary greatly. So will their circumstances. But our attitude must not vary. This is possible only if it is grounded on the unconditional love of God.

Male Counselors

A special problem can arise when a confused, distressed woman mistakes her male counselor's concern for a more personal interest. To protect themselves from an unhealthy dependence, some men remain distant and aloof, an attitude that can easily be interpreted as indifference.

Men don't need to be afraid to show concern for and acceptance of a hurting woman. She needs to know they care. But men should heed the following safeguards:

- Don't be physical. A hug, an arm around her shoulders, or a hand squeeze can be misinterpreted by an already confused and lonely woman. Let words and attitude convey your concern.
- Don't encourage dependence. It feels good to have someone need you, someone to tell you how much your help means to her. But remember, by allowing too much emotional dependence, you are setting up an already hurting woman for even more pain.
- Be especially sensitive, careful to see the problem from the woman's perspective. Infidelity, for instance, is every bit as much a sin for a man as it is for a woman, even though it is not generally viewed that way in Western culture.
- Recognize your prejudices and stereotypes and weed them out. You may think this is not a problem to you, but be careful. Some of our prejudices are deeply ingrained. In a case of wife abuse, for instance, will you be quick to assess the obviously distraught woman's manner as being due to a female tendency toward hysteria? The husband whose demeanor conveys emotional control may try to convince you that she is hysterical.

Know the Resources

Some Christians mistakenly think that they should be able to call on the power of God to immediately deliver anyone from any distress. To rely on psychologists or other professionals, they reason, is unspiritual, a sign of a lack of faith. This is a sad and dangerous mistake. God made us complex beings. Certainly He can heal and restore any aspect of our lives, but He can use various means to accomplish this end. Occasionally He does it miraculously and instantaneously, but more often He uses doctors, public agencies, courts, psychiatrists, psychologists, marriage and family counselors—and time.

As good stewards of the resources God has given, wise counselors will accept every available means of help. This includes both secular and religious resources. We should become acquainted with local agencies and specialists and be prepared to draw on their expertise.

Know Our Limitations

In some instances we ourselves may be able to meet the needs of the women who come to us, although this will probably not be the case with the situations discussed in this book. Sometimes we alone may not be able to provide the necessary help, but the local church body or Christian community can. At other times we will need to find outside help.

For some people, giving advice comes naturally. They pride themselves on being able to intuitively see through to the heart of a difficult situation and to diagnose the underlying cause. If we are like that, we must resist the temptation to "play psychologist." What may seem to us to be a small problem with a simple solution may in fact be just the surface of a very complex condition with deeply embedded, entangled roots. Unless you are specifically trained to diagnose and treat, don't! Leave that to the professionals.

Use God's Word

Clichés and platitudes are worth little. Our own advice may sometimes be good, sometimes not so good. But God's truths are sure and dependable, and they stand forever. As we help those in distress to work through their problems, we can show them what God has to say about similar situations, about sin, and about forgiveness. Allow

14

the Holy Spirit to guide. The words of the prophet Isaiah are as true today as they were when he spoke them many centuries ago: "The grass withers and the flowers fall, but the word of our God stands forever" (Isaiah 40:8).

Professional Counselors

When we need to refer someone to a psychiatrist, a psychologist, a family or marriage counselor, or to another specialist, how do we know whom to recommend? A well-trained, fully competent Christian counselor experienced in the specific field in question would be the person of choice. The problem is that often no such person is available. Don't give up. Spend some time looking at and evaluating those who *are* available. Here are some guidelines to help us in our search:

- If we have to decide between "trained, experienced professional" and "Christian," which should we choose? While it is unwise to make a blanket statement, in most cases the better choice would probably be the trained professional. Often a person who means well ends up compounding a problem by saying and doing the wrong thing. One warning, though: It is extremely important that Christian principles not be undermined by a non-Christian counselor. Before recommending someone, we should make sure that he or she respects and upholds Christian principles.
- We should be sure that the counselors we recommend really are qualified. We can do this by checking their credentials, the professional societies in which they have been accepted, and any national listings in which they are included.
- Experience is another important quality for prospective counselors. A person who has had a great deal of success with couples experiencing marital problems may be totally unable to handle a child molester or an alcoholic. Be straightforward. Ask the counselor, "In what types of situations have you had experience? What do you consider your particular strengths?"
- No one is an expert in all problems. If we live in an area where many professionals are available, we may be able to recommend different people for different situations. But if we live where there are very few professional counselors, we may have to settle for those who are not as well trained or experienced. It is to be hoped they will be willing to make

themselves as knowledgeable as possible on a wide range of problems.

- Take the time to interview counselors before putting them on the recommended list. Ask about their specific experience, their methods of counseling, their religious beliefs, the principles by which they operate, and anything else that might affect their effectiveness.
- If possible, talk with friends or acquaintances who have been in counseling and get the names of professionals with whom they had good experiences.

The purpose of this book is to assist Christian leaders in helping women who turn to them in times of crisis. It is written for nonprofessionals who are willing to reach out and offer help to hurting women.

Each chapter has two main parts: The first deals with information presented in a counseling setting, and the second considers specific counseling aids. The section on counseling aids includes—

- A brief overview of the problem for quick reference
- A list of specific dos and don'ts for counseling
- A resource list containing such information as the names and numbers of crisis agencies, hotlines, organizations from whom further information can be obtained, and a suggested reading list
- A local resource list for the counselor to complete
- In some chapters, suggestions of ways the church can help to meet the needs of women facing particular problems.

Ideally this book should be read straight through. The local reference section should be filled in immediately and updated periodically. There is good reason to do this ahead of time. When we confront a crisis, we can quickly scan the overview, refer to the specific counseling dos and don'ts, and make referrals from our list of references.

Chapter 11 considers a question that we are certain to face: "Why me?" The chapter suggests some specific insights and comforts that we can offer a hurting person. This chapter also deals with the matter of forgiveness—the forgiveness of God, a victim's forgiveness for the one whose sin has caused her great pain and suffering, a sinner's forgiveness for herself, and the forgiveness of Christians for those whose sins have already been erased by God.

One last word of encouragement: We do not have to bear the responsibility of counseling a woman in crisis. The real counselor is the Lord Himself. We are merely His agents, His channels of help and healing. We do, however, have a responsibility to prepare ourselves to be used by Him. When we have done this, we can trust Him to lead us in guiding the wounded, confused, and frightened who come to us for help.

DOS AND DON'TS

The Greek physician Hippocrates said, "As to diseases, make a habit of two things—to help or, at least, to do no harm." This is good advice for crisis counselors, too.

Do ...

- Understand the importance of your attitude toward the person who comes to you for help. Are you truly concerned and willing to do what you can? Or are you annoyed by the interruption, impatient, and uncomfortable? You won't easily hide your true feelings.
- Know your limitations. Leave the diagnosis and treatment to the professionals.
- Guard against overreacting. Expressions of shock, horror, or disgust are hardly comforting to a distressed woman.
- Offer the suffering person compassion, acceptance, and understanding.
- Commend her for her courage, honesty, and willingness to seek help.
- Be willing to speak boldly of things deemed secret and unmentionable.
- Be trustworthy. Unless it is necessary to report specific information of her situation to protect someone, respect the woman's desire for confidentiality.
- Act quickly if you suspect that someone may be in danger. Contact an appropriate professional worker or public authority immediately.
- Encourage the woman to make her own decisions. We can—and certainly should—guide, advise, refer, and point out biblical principles, but we must not make the decisions with which she will have to live.
- Be aware of the special dilemmas facing the victims of wife abuse, child abuse, incest, and molestation.

- Remember that in all your counseling, you are representing Christ.
- Seek God's wisdom. Whenever possible, rely on biblical principles to comfort, encourage, and advise.
- Pray, pray, and pray some more! Pray with the offending person if you can, pray with those who have been hurt, pray alone for everyone involved. Pray for healing and for restoration for all. Pray for wisdom and a forgiving spirit for yourself.
- Assure everyone involved—and believe yourself—that no matter how great the hurt, there is always hope. Our God is a God of miracles.

Don't ...

- Minimize the problem.
- Depend on platitudes and easy, simplistic answers. For some of the situations covered in this book, the woman involved may very well find herself "between a rock and a hard place." For every problem there is a solution, but the road to finding it may be long, hard, and painful.
- Be too quick to blame the suffering person for her problems. She may be the guilty party, but often there is much more involved than there appears to be.
- Compromise standards. Sin is sin, however it is rationalized. Our accepting the person need not imply condoning her sin. Following the example of Christ, we are to hate the sin but love the sinner.
- Be judgmental. This attitude declares that the person herself is good or bad instead of evaluating the impact of the deed.
- Show embarrassment, shame, disgust, impatience, or other emotions that will make it more difficult—perhaps impossible—for her to talk to you about her problems.
- Automatically assume that a person who has fallen into sin is not a child of God. The same problems exist among Christians as among non-Christians.
- Try to diagnosis or treat beyond your ability.
- Advise Christians to endure abuse in the hopes of keeping their families together. Telling victims of wife abuse, child molestation, child abuse, or incest to "go home and keep praying" can be dangerous advice; it can even be fatal.
- Tell the woman that what has happened in her life is "the cross you must bear" patiently and without complaint.

- Consider it unspiritual, or a symptom of a lack of faith, to seek professional psychological or physiological help.
- Discourage either the victim or the victimized from seeing professionals, either by word or by attitude.
- Make the mistake of thinking that grief and pain are a denial of one's faith in God and His sovereignty.
- Give medical advice, make medical diagnoses, or give any advice about medications. If there appear to be medical implications to a specific situation, refer the woman to a physician.
- Give legal advice. Refer her to an attorney.
- Try to counsel in your own power. Instead, wait on the Lord.

SUGGESTED READING

Adams, Jay E. *The Christian Counselor's Manual.* Phillipsburg, N.J.: Presbyterian and Reformed, 1973.

Christenson, Evelyn. *Gaining Through Losing.* Wheaton, Ill.: Victor Books.

Crabb, Lawrence J., Jr. *Effective Biblical Counseling.* Grand Rapids: Zondervan, 1977.

Dobson, James C. *Love Must Be Tough.* Waco: Word Books, 1983.

Hoekema, Anthony A. *The Christian Looks At Himself.* Grand Rapids: Eerdmans, 1975.

Hughes, Selwyn. *Helping People Through Their Problems,* Minneapolis: Bethany House, 1982.

Somerville, Robert. *Help for Hotliners.* Phillipsburg, N.J.: Presbyterian and Reformed, 1978.

This book includes instructions for setting up and operating a hotline counseling service and a bibliography for further study.

Wright, Norm. *Training Christians to Counsel.* Eugene, Ore.: Harvest House, 1984.

HOW CAN THE CHRISTIAN COMMUNITY HELP?

Christian Professionals. When we are making our lists of local references, we should include as many Christians as we feel are qualified (doctors, attorneys, psychiatrists, psychologists, marriage counselors, family counselors).

Education. Before the Christian community can help, they must be acquainted with the problems that are prevalent in our society. They must also understand and accept the fact that these problems affect their Christian brothers and sisters as well as the Christian spouses of non-Christians. For some, this may be a real revelation.

Encouragement. People who are willing to stand by those who are hurt and suffering are desperately needed. Hurting people need Christians who are willing to listen when they need to talk, to cry with them in their pain, to appreciate their progress, to be there as they struggle to rebuild their broken lives.

Emergency Prayer Lines. A prayer line should be made up of people who truly believe in the power of prayer and are committed to a prayer ministry. When the problem is a sensitive one, the people need not be told the details or the identity of those involved. A call for prayer can simply state, "A young woman needs you to pray about a difficult family situation. Especially remember her two children."

Forgiveness. The body of Christ needs to understand and practice true forgiveness. This is dealt with in chapter 11.

Support Groups. If a hurting person is able to get in touch with others who have gone through the same problem, it will be of great help. You might keep a list of Christians who have struggled with specific problems and are willing to share with and encourage others who encounter the same struggle.

LOCAL REFERENCES

SUPPORT GROUPS

A group of loving, concerned Christian women who will pray with, listen to, comfort, and support the victims of tragedies or problems.

NAME:

Number:

Notes:

NAME:

Number:

Notes:

NAME:

Number:

Notes:

NAME:

Number:

Notes:

PHYSICIANS

Medical doctors who are sensitive to the conditions of depressed women, or those who may have other physical considerations.

NAME:

Number:

Notes:

NAME:

Number:

Notes:

NAME:

Number:

Notes:

PSYCHIATRISTS, PSYCHOLOGISTS, TRAINED COUNSELORS

NAME:

Number:

Notes:

NAME:

Number:

Notes:

NAME:

Number:

Notes:

2.

Alcohol and Drug Abuse

"You have been here for twenty minutes now, Marilyn, and I still have no idea what you want to talk to me about," you say evenly, trying hard to hide the exasperation and impatience you feel. "When your husband called to set up this appointment, he said you had a problem you needed to discuss with me. Isn't it time you told me what it is?"

The middle-aged homemaker who has been sitting sullenly across the desk from you ever since she arrived suddenly springs to life. "There is nothing wrong with me!" she snaps. "The so-called problem only exists in Fred's mind. He wants me to tell you I have a drinking problem. In fact, he's gotten it into his mind that I'm an alcoholic. The whole idea is ridiculous! I don't know why he has to get so worked up about nothing!"

You look closely at Marilyn. She looks little different from many other women in your church. She certainly doesn't *look* like an alcoholic. But then, what does an alcoholic look like? Only 5 percent fit the stereotype of a gutter-sleeping derelict. The National Institute of Alcohol and Alcohol Abuse estimates that fully half of the problem drinkers in this country are women, many of them quite successful at hiding their addiction. Could Marilyn be one of them?

After a good deal of pressing and prodding, Marilyn finally admits to the events that led up to her husband's call. "Every morning after Fred leaves for work and the kids are off to school I enjoy a couple of drinks. It gets me started in the morning, wakes me up, you might say. Well, yesterday Fred came back home to get some papers he forgot and caught me before I could hide the bottle. When I admitted that I drink every morning, he got upset and insisted that I have a problem. I tried to explain that I'm not an addict or anything—I mean, I don't *need* the drink, I just enjoy it. But he wouldn't believe me. He started looking back at every little thing that has gone wrong lately, and he blamed them all on my 'drinking problem.' "

By her own admission Marilyn drinks alone every morning. She says she does not need the drinks, yet she also says they "wake her

23

up" and "get her started." As Marilyn continues to talk, it becomes more and more evident that many of those "little things that have gone wrong lately" really were due to her drinking: forgotten appointments, minor car accidents, frequent illness, missing money.

Some of the warning signs of alcoholism are doing things when drinking that are later regretted, trying unsuccessfully to control the drinking, taking five or more drinks a day, problems with family or friends or at work over drinking, and two or more blackouts while drinking. Because she is uncooperative, you don't know how many of these characteristics apply to Marilyn. But according to many experts, the definition of an alcoholic is one whose drinking interferes with one or more aspect of her life. Using that definition, Marilyn certainly is an alcoholic, one of an estimated ten million in this country.

It is important to understand that 95 percent of America's alcoholics are not skid-row bums. They don't wear worn-out, dirty clothes, nor do they sleep in gutters while hugging wine bottles. Most are more like Marilyn: respectable family people, working men and women, upstanding members of the community, even church members.

A great deal has been written on the cause of alcoholism: Is an alcoholic's fate predetermined by heredity? Is it a disease, or is it a learned condition? The truth is probably a combination of all these. Dr. Nicholas A. Pace, assistant professor of clinical medicine at the New York University School of Medicine, states, "With a lot of drinking and a little neglect, almost anyone can develop the disease we call alcoholism, just as any of us can contract pneumonia by foolishly exposing ourselves to its causes. While some people are more susceptible than others, it is dangerous for anyone to hope for some kind of built-in immunity."

The place a person falls on any chart of alcoholic predisposition is not really the determining factor. By drinking long and hard enough, a person on the low end of the scale can still become an alcoholic, while someone who is very high on the scale but doesn't drink will never be affected.

To induce her to acknowledge her problem, you decide to be straightforward with Marilyn. Leaning toward her and looking her straight in the eye you ask, "Marilyn, is your drinking interfering with your life?"

Fidgeting and shifting uncomfortably in her chair, Marilyn tries hard to avoid your steady gaze. But because you know that nothing can be done to help her until she admits her problem, you are insistent.

"Yes," she finally answers quietly. And suddenly, as if the floodgates had finally swung open, the whole story pours out.

Marilyn's morning drinking has been going on for two years and getting progressively worse. In the last few months it has gotten so bad that she can barely drag herself out of bed in the morning. Her only thought is to get Fred and the children out of the house as quickly as possible so that she can get herself a drink to "wake up." But one drink always leads to another, then another, then another. By noon she is usually asleep on the couch. Although she has always managed to rouse herself enough to prepare dinner, she feels awful and constantly nags at the children. Her children are finding more and more reason to stay away from home in afternoons and evenings. But on weekends someone is always around. For Marilyn, weekends are pure torture.

By nature a very active and outgoing person, Marilyn has dropped out of every organization in which she was formerly involved. She has separated herself from all her friends. She is still attending church, she says, because it's the one thing that allows her to preserve a sense of normalcy about her life.

You ask Marilyn if she has ever tried to stop drinking. She admits that she has. "So many nights I have lain in bed making myself the same promise: 'Tomorrow will be different. Tomorrow I won't take a single drink.' But by the next morning I felt so bad that I thought, 'Just one drink to wake me up. Just one and no more.'" With a sigh she adds, "I guess I don't have much willpower."

Marilyn doesn't understand that willpower has nothing to do with it. The fact is, alcoholics cannot will themselves to give up liquor. In times of desperation they will make all kinds of promises. And when they swear they won't get drunk again, they really do mean it. But every well-intentioned promise is sure to be broken. Alcoholics just don't have the ability to stop alone.

"At least I'm not on drugs," Marilyn says. "That would be a problem. If it was drugs I'd *really* be an addict."

What Marilyn doesn't understand is that she already is a drug addict. Alcohol is a drug that causes physical dependence. That's why drug and alcohol use are so often lumped together under the heading "substance abuse." People who are abusing drugs show changes in their behavior. They tend to become withdrawn and to lose interest in activities that formerly interested them. They may have trouble concentrating and have a tendency to oversleep. All these symptoms are similar to those found in alcoholics.

What are Marilyn's prospects for attaining an alcohol-free life? That depends. If she comes to the point of finally acknowledging her problem, and if she truly wants to change, her prospects for recovery are excellent. But if she is only cooperating because Fred has forced her to, it is unlikely that healing will come. Alcoholism is by no means a hopeless condition, but it cannot be treated until it is acknowledged. Like any other alcoholic, Marilyn's chances of recovery depend on and begin with one person—the alcoholic herself.

"I feel better than I have in a long, long time," Marilyn tells you. "I just know that things are going to be different from now on!"

Evidently she is expecting you to make a few suggestions, to pray with her, then to send her on her way. But healing does not come so easily. Marilyn needs professional treatment. The nature and length of that treatment will depend on the seriousness of her addiction. However acute the symptoms of an alcoholic, there is a program capable of dealing with them. There is no such thing as a hopeless alcoholic.

Where Treatment Begins

Most alcoholic treatment programs provide a combination of services. A person who is addicted to alcohol first of all needs to recover from the acute effects the drug has had on her body. This procedure of ridding the body of alcohol and allowing it to adjust to doing without it is called detoxification. But detoxification must be followed up with a counseling program.

For alcoholics, any program is only a treatment program. There is no such thing as a cure. Never again can alcoholics drink without risk. For the rest of their lives, they must be total abstainers.

When faced with his wife's drinking, Fred called you for an appointment and told Marilyn to go in and get help with her problem. Marilyn kept the appointment. But what if she hadn't? Or what if she should now refuse to cooperate with a treatment program? Is there anything more her concerned husband can do?

Spouses cannot make alcoholics get well. Since the effects of alcoholism make addicts helpless to control their drinking, it does no good to nag, complain, beg, berate, or embarrass. Condemning their drinking as a sin, scolding and shaming them, threatening them—

none of these help, because alcoholics are powerless to help themselves. Even if a spouse succeeds in forcing the drinker into counseling or a treatment program, the effort is doomed to failure unless the addict truly wants help.

It is commonly thought that alcoholics cannot be helped until they hit bottom. Fortunately that's not true. Today the stress is on getting people into treatment before they lose their jobs and families and cause irreparable damage to their bodies.

Before alcoholics can move toward recovery, they must accept the responsibility for their drinking. They must be held accountable for all their actions, whether drunk or sober. Many alcoholics are quick to find someone else to blame—their spouses, their parents, their bosses—sometimes even God Himself. They keep right on drinking to excess no matter what, and it is never their fault.

At first Marilyn wouldn't even admit that there was a problem, yet it later became apparent that she actually had been concerned about her drinking. Fred's pushing encouraged her to face the truth. In other cases it may be much harder to persuade the drinker to admit the problem. This is hardly surprising when we consider that the alcoholic's entire thought process is based on denial and self-deception. Moreover, alcoholics can hardly be expected to be capable of clear and rational decisions regarding their well-being. Concerned spouses who intend to wait until the drinkers admit their problem and ask for help will likely wait forever. Every year thousands of alcoholics die without ever admitting that anything was wrong.

A Family Problem

Fred sees alcohol as Marilyn's problem. While it is true that she is the drinker, the problem is not hers alone. Alcoholism is a family problem, and the entire family needs to be involved in the treatment.

In groups such as Al-Anon, family members learn how to remove the support system that holds the alcoholic's life together. It is the "enabler"—the person who covers the alcoholic's irresponsibilities, thereby prolonging and worsening the problem—who makes it possible for her to keep up the appearance of normalcy. Enablers need to learn how to give ultimatums that will force the drinkers to admit the problem, to force them to accept the consequences of their drinking. Yet this is not something that should be attempted alone. Without the guidance of someone trained in dealing with alcoholics, a well-meaning family can end up pushing the alcoholic even further away from help and healing.

27

In the end, if Marilyn steadfastly refuses to accept help, Fred will find himself faced with some very tough decisions. Is he willing to stay with her? If so, he should definitely get help for himself and their children. On the other hand, an ultimatum laying out the circumstances under which the family is willing to stay with her may very well be the thing that will motivate Marilyn to get the help she needs.

Teenage Alcoholism

Increasingly the person who comes to a counselor seeking help for an alcoholic problem comes neither for herself nor her spouse. She comes distraught over her child who is abusing alcohol or other drugs. We have all heard the shocking statistics of drug use among teenagers and even children in elementary school. We hear less about their use of alcohol, but their problem is no less frightening. In 1980 the Surgeon General reported that the mortality rate for young people had increased 11 percent. Most of this increase was related to drugs and alcohol.

Furthermore, in a study performed by the Department of Health and Human Services, 19 percent of youths fourteen to nineteen years old were experiencing problems related to the use of alcohol. Even more amazing, about a third of the half-million American fourth-graders responding to a recent survey said that drinking beer or liquor was a "big problem" among their age group. The survey also showed that 30 percent sensed pressure to try alcoholic drinks.

It is well-known that adolescence is the age of rebellion, the age of experimentation. It's the time when kids are beginning to break away from their families. Though they are young and inexperienced, they think they know everything. At this age the values and opinions of friends are more important to them than those of their parents.

Substance abuse among young people has reached epidemic proportions. A wise parent will know the warning signals and be alert for them. Also, they must appreciate the power of peer pressure on even the most mature and well-adjusted teenager.

One of the great myths of our time is that only parents who don't really care about their children, those who neglect or abuse them, have youngsters who get addicted to drugs and alcohol. The myth holds that it is not a problem of good parents and good kids, certainly not of Christian families. How wrong this is!

Like adult alcoholics, addicted children can be treated successfully. This treatment and support is every bit as important to their recovery as it is for adults.

You may have very strong personal opinions on the causes, curses, and cures of alcoholism and drug dependence. You may also have strong feelings about the people who have put themselves into a position to become addicted. But as a counselor, remember that you cannot make a person change. Neither can anyone in her family. But God can. No case is hopeless. What good news you have to share!

A QUICK OVERVIEW

Alcoholism and drug abuse are by no means hopeless conditions, but they cannot be successfully treated until the problem is acknowledged by the addicted person. Admitting their helplessness is an extremely difficult thing for alcoholics and drug addicts to do.

Since the effects of alcoholism and the dependence caused by drugs make their victims helpless to control their actions, it does no good to nag, complain, beg, berate, or embarrass them.

It is the "enabler"—the person who covers the addict's irresponsibilities and in so doing allows the problem to continue— that keeps the alcoholic's life together. It is when her life begins to fall apart that the addict is finally pushed to seek help. Therefore the family's cooperation is essential in the treatment of the addicted person.

Whether we are approached by the victim herself, or by a concerned spouse or parent, our job is to do everything we can to induce the addict to admit the problem, to agree to get help, and to cooperate with the treatment prescribed.

DOS AND DON'TS

If the person involved in drug or alcohol abuse comes to us herself, it will probably be right after she has suffered a severe problem that was a direct result of her drinking. This is the best time for us to talk to her, for then she is most likely to follow our recommendations.

If the problem drinker is forced or coerced into coming to us, our attempts to help will probably be unsuccessful. We are working against a powerful denial system based not only on the frightening stigma attached to alcoholism or drug abuse, but also on the strength of the physical dependence. The woman may well feel that she *can't* stop drinking, that it simply isn't possible. Therefore, for us to ask her to stop drinking may seem like an impossible demand, regardless of the damage the alcohol is doing. Our job as crisis counselors will be to do all we can to persuade her to recognize and admit the problem and agree to treatment.

Do ...

- Encourage the family members to stop covering up for the problems the drugs or alcohol are causing the abuser. Remind them that they must allow her to take the responsibility for and to suffer the consequences of her drinking.
- Be straightforward and nonjudgmental when discussing the problem with the abuser.
- Be willing to cooperate with secular sources. Alcoholics Anonymous, for instance, has an outstanding rate of success. This organization has much to offer that few churches can match.
- Avoid the word "alcoholism." It is overly threatening to many people and is not necessarily accurate. Not every heavy drinker or binge drinker is an alcoholic. A better term to use is "problem drinker" or "uncontrolled drinker."
- Stress that addiction is not a hopeless situation. Help is available.
- Help her family to understand that this is not just her problem; it is a family problem.
- Remember that it is unlikely that the problem of addiction will be resolved without professional help.
- Encourage her to look long and hard at herself and her life. Try to induce her to acknowledge her problem.
- Encourage the family to pursue treatment even without the consent and cooperation of the drinker. Perhaps their action will cause her to face the truth about her problem.
- Enlist the help of recovered alcoholics or drug users within the church or Christian community. Recovering abusers relate better to others "who have been there."
- Let her know that you care about her and are concerned about her and her family.
- Pray with the distressed family and encourage them to commit the problem to the Lord.
- Set up an effective burden-bearing society in the church that will give any hurting person or family the loving support God intended us to offer each other.
- Understand, and let the victim know you believe, that despite

her problem she is a worthwhile person whom God loves deeply. It is God's will that she be healed, and He will help her toward that end if she will let Him.

Don't ...

- Act shocked at anything the abuser or her family says.
- Try to make a medical diagnosis. Refer the person to a professional.
- Try to diagnose the underlying cause of the problem. We may think we know why she is hooked, but remember, diagnosing is not in our crisis counseling job description.
- Moralize, scold, or berate the abuser.
- Assume a lecturing or preaching tone of voice.
- Be condemning in words, tone of voice, or manner. Condemnation on our part will immediately turn the abuser off to anything we have to say.
- Tell her to use a little self-control and stop drinking. An alcoholic cannot do it.
- Be misled by sympathy-evoking tactics of the abuser. Alcoholics are adept at playing on the sympathy of others.
- Ever "cover up" for the alcoholic or drug abuser. A misguided "kindness" or "helping hand" can lead to a serious delay in the person's getting the real help she desperately needs.
- Discuss the problem with anyone except the family or professionals who are in a position to offer help.
- Let secular groups usurp the place of the church. They are valuable, useful tools, but they are not a substitute for the fellowship of the body of Christ.

When a woman comes on behalf of her uncooperative alcohol or drug abusing spouse, suggest that she ...

- Learn all she can about substance abuse.
- Retain hope.
- Pray. Together ask the Lord specifically to bring her husband to the point of admitting his addiction and a desire to seek help. Pray also for the protection and strengthening of the family.
- Attend a support group for families of substance abusers such as Al-Anon.
- Obtain information on treatment centers—admission require-

ments, cost, services available, time commitment—so that she will have it available if her husband decides to cooperate.

- Refrain from nagging, begging, pleading with, or berating her husband. Remind her that he has lost his capacity for voluntary action.
- No longer keep his life together for him. Encourage her to stop covering for him, lying for him, paying his bills, and generally covering for his irresponsibility. The longer she covers for him, the longer it will be before her husband is forced to accept the responsibility for his addiction.
- Not protect him from the consequences of any illegal actions, such as drug possession or driving while intoxicated. Let him know that if he chooses to break the law he will have to live with the consequences.
- Not blame herself for the addiction of her spouse or child. It is not her fault.

RESOURCES

Hotline. A national drug and alcohol abuse hotline can be reached by calling this toll-free number: 1–800–BE–SOBER.

Cocaine Treatment. There is a special toll-free number for people with cocaine problems. The number is: 1–800–COCAINE.

Treatment Centers. Alcohol and drug abuse treatment centers have sprung up all over the country and are having considerable success. The average hospital stay is two to three weeks.

Alcoholics Anonymous. There is a branch of Alcoholics Anonymous in almost every city and town across the United States. People who attend are made to feel welcome and comfortable from the time they first arrive. One of AA's main tenets is: It takes an alcoholic to help an alcoholic. Everyone there has been addicted to alcohol, and there are always plenty of people willing to help. Meetings are free. The headquarters for Alcoholics Anonymous is:

> Alcoholics Anonymous World Services
> P.O. Box 459, Grand Central Station
> New York, NY 10017

Although Alcoholics Anonymous places strong emphasis on God and the necessity of depending on Him, it is not a Christian group. It is a very helpful organization, but it must not take the place of the church; its support and friendship must not take the place of fellowship in the body of Christ.

Alcoholics Victorious. This is an international fellowship of Christian alcoholics with more than a hundred chapters throughout the world. Founded on Christian principles, this group is committed to helping alcoholics overcome their problems through God's strength and faith in Jesus Christ. For more information, contact:

> Charles Stegman
> Alcoholics Victorious
> 123 South Green Street
> Chicago, IL 60607

Al-Anon. This is a support group for families who have to cope with an alcoholic relative. Associated with Alcoholics Anonymous, it also has chapters all over the country. Their headquarters are located at:

> Al-Anon Family Group Headquarters
> P.O. Box 183, Madison Square Garden
> New York, NY 10017

Alateen. This is the teenage division of Al-Anon. It is specifically intended for young people with alcoholic parents. Its headquarters has the same address as Al-Anon.

National Clearinghouse for Alcohol Information. This organization offers a number of free services and products. It provides referrals on request as well as directories of treatment resources for each of the fifty states. It can be contacted at:

> P.O. Box 2345
> Rockville, MD 20852
> Telephone: (301) 468–2600

National Council of Alcoholism. The council will assist in locating the best program for an individual alcoholic. It has chapters throughout the country. Its headquarters are located at:

> 733 Third Avenue
> New York, NY 10017

Recovery, Inc. Similar to Alcoholics Anonymous, though not as well-known, this organization for alcoholics has branches around the country. It also provides ongoing emotional support for relatives of alcoholics.

Other Agencies. Help may also be available through agencies such as the Jewish Board of Family and Children's Services, Catholic Charities, or the Salvation Army. Check the telephone directory for local numbers.

SUGGESTED READING

Costales, Claire, and Jo Berry. *Staying Dry: A Workable Solution to the Problem of Alcohol Abuse.* Ventura, Calif.: Regal Books, 1983.

DeJong, Alexander C. *Help and Hope for the Alcoholic.* Wheaton, Ill.: Tyndale House, 1982.

A book, written by a pastor who conquered alcoholism, that has insights for friends and family members of alcoholics.

Dobson, James. *Love Must Be Tough.* Waco, Tex.: Word Books, 1983.

Drews, Toby Rice. *Getting Them Sober.* South Plainfield, N.J.: Bridge Publishers, 1980.

A guide for those who live with an alcoholic.

Dunn, Jerry C. *God Is for the Alcoholic.* Chicago: Moody Press, 1967.

A Christ-centered solution to the problem of alcoholism written by a recovered alcoholic and containing sections on understanding the alcoholic, ways to help the alcoholic, and ways the alcoholic can help himself.

Hughes, Harold. *The Honorable Alcoholic.* Grand Rapids: Zondervan, 1983.

The autobiography of a former U.S. Senator.

Nale, Sharon. *A Cry for Help.* Philadelphia: Fortress, 1982.

A book that includes many resources and information.

Neff, Pauline. *Tough Love: How Parents Can Deal With Drug Abuse.* Nashville: Abingdon, 1982.

A book for parents whose children are now on drugs or are exposed drug users, with the author's proposal of a cure for drug abusers and positive support for their families.

Ohlemacher, Janet. *Beloved Alcoholic: What to Do When a Family Member Drinks.* Grand Rapids: Zondervan, 1984.

A personal story of one family's involvement with alcoholism, describing the "alcoholic family," inspiration and guidance, programs to bring alcoholics to recovery, and the ultimate step—legal commitment.

Rehrer, Ronald L. *Now What Do I Do?* St. Louis: Concordia, 1982.

A guide for young people dealing with problems of drugs and drinking that considers moods and feelings, peer pressure, parental response, and church teachings, and suggests Christ-centered alternatives.

Strack, Jay. *Drugs and Drinking: The All-American Cop-Out.* Nashville: Thomas Nelson, 1979.

The health and social dangers of alcohol and drug abuse among the young, with helpful facts and a plan of action.

Other Resources

Al-Anon has a number of books and pamphlets available. Some of the titles are *Living with an Alcoholic, The Dilemma of the Alcoholic Marriage, One Day at a Time in Al-Anon.*

For a complete literature catalog and price list write:

Al-Anon Family Group Headquarters, Inc.
P.O. Box 182, Madison Square Station
New York, New York 10159

Peale, Norman Vincent. *Roads to Recovery.*

Accounts told in *Guideposts* fashion of people who have dealt effectively with problem drinking, with topics such as If You Drink, If Your Child Drinks, If You've Kicked Your Drinking Habit, plus tips by Norman Vincent Peale on how to use the booklet. Available for fifty cents from:

Guideposts
Carmel, New York 10512

Help for the Alcoholic is a ninety-minute cassette tape available from:

Focus on the Family
Box 500
Arcadia, CA 91006

LOCAL REFERENCES

LOCAL HOTLINE

Number:

MEDICAL DOCTOR

NAME:

Number:

ALCOHOL TREATMENT PROGRAM

Number:

Notes:

ALCOHOLICS ANONYMOUS

Number:

Notes:

AL-ANON FAMILY GROUPS

Number:

Notes:

RECOVERY, INC.

Number:

Notes:

OTHER SERVICES FOR ALCOHOL AND DRUG ABUSE

NAME:

Number:

Notes:

NAME:

Number:

36

Notes:

NAME:

Number:

Notes:

Because alcoholics and drug abusers tend to respond better to people who have faced similar experiences, it would be helpful to enlist the help of Christians who have recovered from addiction. Ask them ahead of time if they would be willing to participate in such a program, and keep their names and phone numbers near at hand.

NAME:

Number:

Comments:

NAME:

Number:

Comments:

NAME:

Number:

Comments:

3.   *Child Abuse*

When you heard about the accident you went to see Jonathon in the hospital. His family was new in the neighborhood, and Jonathon and his mother had visited your church once or twice. You were surprised at how badly the little boy was hurt—broken ribs, fractured arm, face black and blue. The injuries seemed rather widespread and severe for a tumble down the stairs.

You took a stuffed dog to Jonathon, talked to him for a few minutes, and expressed your sympathies to his distraught mother. "Let me know if there's anything I can do," you said, because that's always a good thing to say.

That was two days ago. Now Jonathon's mother is on the telephone to you. "I did it," she says, her voice shaking. "I hurt my son!"

Without giving you a chance to respond, she blurts out the whole story.

"I had such a hard day at work. All I wanted to do was go home, get Jonathon to bed, and have a little time to myself. I made it through dinner, dishes, and bathtime. Then it was bedtime, but Jonathon just wouldn't go to bed. I scolded, I pleaded, I cajoled, I threatened, but he was in a bad mood and just kept whining. Then we made a deal: I would make him a cup of hot chocolate, and he would go right to sleep with no more fooling around.

"Well, I made the chocolate as I said I would, but Jonathon still wasn't satisfied. He complained that it was too hot and he wouldn't drink it. By then I had had it with him. I said if he didn't drink that chocolate immediately, I'd pour it on his head! He started drinking, all right, but then he dropped the mug and spilled chocolate all over his bed.

"As I stared down at the chocolate-soaked bedding, something suddenly snapped inside me. In an uncontrollable fury I started hitting my little boy again and again and again. The next thing I remember I was standing over him at the bottom of the stairs. I guess I had dragged him out of his room and thrown him down the stairs."

The Untold Story

Child abuse is very much in the news these days. Headlines and articles recount the short, sad lives of children who are subjected to all kinds of savage torture. What those headlines don't tell about are the little ones all across the country whose suffering remains hidden. Their bodies are bruised and broken and their spirits are battered, but no one outside the family realizes what is happening to them.

It is estimated that every year one million American children are the victims of serious physical abuse or neglect, mostly by their own parents. Moreover, studies show that parents cause the death of at least two thousand children annually. Because practically all offenders deny that they are abusive, many child-abuse incidents, like Jonathon's, are disguised as accidents. How many victims there actually are is unknown, for the majority of incidents are never reported.

What the experts do know is that even the reported cases are far too numerous and that the cost in physical and emotional suffering and ruined lives is intolerable in a civilized society. Even more intolerable is the fact that child abuse perpetuates itself. In most cases—some estimates run as high as 90 percent—the abusive parent was also abused as a child.

"Jonathon and I just moved here," his mother explains. "I don't know anyone in town. My husband's transfer won't come through for a couple of months, but I thought I should go ahead and move so that Jonathon would be here for the start of the school year. Unfortunately, we didn't count on the high cost of maintaining two households, and I ended up having to get a job immediately. I work hard and get very little pay. When I come home in the evening, I'm always exhausted."

Most people believe that child abuse is a problem mainly among city dwellers, the uneducated, and welfare recipients. It isn't. While it is true that the environmental and family stresses associated with low income contribute to the problem, according to the report of the Justice Department task force, child abuse occurs in every social and economic class and in every neighborhood. It even happens in Christian homes.

Too often when parents are in despair about their own lives, it is their children, the most vulnerable members of our society, who end up being the targets of their frustration. Like Jonathon's mother, most parents who lose control and abuse their children have other problems in their lives—financial or marital troubles, unsatisfactory jobs, loneliness.

Raising children *can* be frustrating and at times exasperating. Spilled milk, wet beds, crying in the middle of the night—these can be trying to the most loving of parents. But in some mothers and fathers, these everyday problems can trigger uncontrollable outbursts of violence.

Some specialists are convinced that, given enough stress, any parent is potentially an abusive parent. Far from being hardened criminals, most mothers and fathers who harm their children are simply overwhelmed by pressures they cannot handle. While some parents are so seriously disturbed that their children's lives are in constant danger, most function normally until they are pushed beyond their limits. When this happens, parenting becomes an unbearable task, and they are unable to cope with the ordinary stresses and strains that come with parenthood.

Studies show that women are more likely to be child abusers than men. The reason is that women usually spend far more time with their children and thus are provoked to a greater degree. With single mothers, the stress of child rearing is often aggravated by financial difficulties and the lack of a supporting adult to share the burdens of parenting.

You ask Jonathon's mother if she has ever hit her son before. She says she has. You ask if her husband was aware of what was happening. She says he was.

"I've never before hurt Jonathon this badly, though," she quickly adds. "When my husband was at home, he would calm me down when I got too frustrated or angry. Of course, most of the time he wasn't home. Sometimes I would see him looking at a bruise on Jonathon. Later he'd ask the boy if he had made me angry, but my husband never said much to me."

In a two-parent family, rarely is only one parent involved in the abuse of a child. Although one is typically the active abuser, the other is a passive abuser in that he or she allows the abuse to continue. Because the drive to punish is beyond their recognition and control, many parents simply cannot call for help as Jonathon's mother did. Unless they are reported by someone else, these abusers will continue to batter their children.

Discipline or Abuse?

"I have to discipline him!" the mother tells you earnestly. "I know I went too far this time. I lost control. But it is my responsibility as a Christian to keep my son in line."

Surprisingly, Christians are some of the most difficult people to convince that child abuse exists to any serious degree. Many feel that anyone who speaks out against child abuse is against spanking and therefore against the Bible. The problem is that some parents are driven by such an out-of-control spare-the-rod-and-spoil-the-child philosophy that they truly believe abusive punishment is the only way to discipline their children properly. Many of these parents argue that as children they were beaten or strapped and that the experience, though painful, was "good for them." This idea is reinforced by some Christian leaders, one of whom tells parents, "Welts and bruises are a sign that you are doing a good job."

As counselors, is it possible for us to draw a line between a disciplining smack and an act of abuse? It isn't easy. One expert offers this guideline: "If an hour after the spanking you can see a red mark, or if a bruise appears, you have crossed the line between discipline and abuse." The goal of discipline is loving guidance, not injury.

You ask the woman on the telephone to tell you as honestly as she can just how she feels about her son.

"Well, at times he can be the sweetest little fellow in the world," she says, "but at other times he is so whining and demanding that I can hardly stand him. When he gets me upset, everything he does makes me furious. I try to reason with him and tell him that he makes me angry when he's so bad. But then he's always been that way, even when he was a baby. And as he gets older, instead of getting better he gets worse. Why does he want to be so bad?"

A better question would be, why would Jonathon persist in behavior that is sure to end in a painful punishment? There are several sensible answers. For one thing, in some ways he is simply behaving like a child. No one, either child or adult, is happy and in a good mood all the time, but adults are better than children at hiding their feelings. Another possibility is that, having repeatedly been told that he is bad ever since infancy, Jonathon may simply be living up to his mother's expectations. Or his naughtiness may be an attempt to get some attention from his mother. Perhaps in Jonathon's mind the only thing worse than being beaten for being bad is receiving no attention at all. This is true for many battered children.

You think back to the conversation you had with Jonathon in the hospital. When you asked him how he happened to fall down the stairs, he said that he was just clumsy. The two of you were alone in the room at the time. Why, you ask his mother, didn't Jonathon give you a hint that something was wrong?

"Oh, he has never said anything to anyone about me hitting him," she tells you. "He always supports what I say. I think he understands that it is at least partly his fault. Anyway, he seems to very quickly forget what has happened."

The fact that someone in Jonathon's situation doesn't tell is not uncommon. Many battered kids don't. Like Jonathon, they often think that the abuse is their fault and is punishment they deserve. They are harder on themselves than they are on their abusive parents. Many abused children actively protect their parents. Sometimes this is because they are afraid of what will happen to them if they tell the truth, but it cannot always be so easily explained. Many children keep right on lying for their parents even after they have been taken out of the home.

Some children, especially older ones, try to let adults know what is happening to them, but too often their attempts are brushed aside. No counselor who is approached by a child, or who is told of abuse by another adult in whom a child has confided, should easily dismiss the subject. Rarely will a child lie about abuse. Accusing troubled children of exaggerating, minimizing the problem by telling them that all kids have trouble at home, or insisting that their parents love them and are just trying to do what is best for them does not offer a solution. Learning that adults are of no help, those children will very likely not try to reach out again.

Whether or not they tell, one thing is certain: Children who are abused by their parents never forget what has happened to them. This abuse becomes a permanent part of who and what they are. This truth should be made abundantly clear to abusive parents.

"I don't want to be a bad mother," the woman says earnestly. "I'm doing the best I can. But sometimes I just can't help myself."

Breaking the Cycle

It has often been said that parenting, the most important job most adults ever have to do, is the one thing in our society for which there is little training and no test for proficiency. No instruction manual comes with the baby. People learn to parent from observing their own parents. If their parents were supportive, loving, and God-fearing, they will most likely be the same way. But if their parents were violent, critical, and impatient, that is how they will most likely raise their own children. In classic fashion the battered child has been programmed for the role of punitive parent. When a mother beats her little one, she is responding in the same way her mother responded to her.

In every instance of child battering, there are two victims: the child and the parent. By helping the troubled parent we are also helping the child.

Most mothers and fathers want to be good parents. They want their children to have a better life than they had. For many who lack proper parenting skills, all that is needed is some good training. Once they understand how they should respond to their children and learn how to react properly, they find that they are generally able to be the kind of parents they want to be. Parenting classes and support groups are wonderful services in which Christian groups and churches can be involved. What an investment in the lives of people for generations to come!

Of course, some battering parents need far more help than a support group can give. There are many therapy clinics, treatment centers, public agencies, and private groups dedicated to helping abusive parents learn to become positive and supportive. There are also many professionals in private practice who are trained to assist parents who cannot control their violence toward their children. As crisis counselors, we should become acquainted with the groups and professionals available where we live, and with their general philosophies and approaches. Only then will we be in a position to make wise, appropriate referrals.

When you suggest that she talk with a professional who can help her learn to deal more positively with her son, Jonathon's mother is silent. When she does finally speak, her voice is strained. "It's not that big a problem," she says. "I see what I've done to Jonathon, how I've hurt him, and it won't happen again. The problem is a thing of the past."

It is obvious that Jonathon's mother is concerned about her son's well-being. There is no doubt that she sincerely wants never again to lose control and hurt him. What she doesn't understand is that this problem will not go away by itself. She admitted that the problem has been growing; without help it will keep growing worse. The next time Jonathon might well be permanently injured—or even killed.

The developmental effects of abuse on a youngster can be devastating. We know that little victims grow up to be big offenders—the child abusers, rapists, prostitutes, alcoholics, and drug addicts of tomorrow. One study shows that more than 90 percent of the inmates at San Quentin Prison were abused as children.

"You aren't going to tell anyone about this, are you?" the woman asks anxiously. "I mean, they might try to take Jonathon away from me. If that happened, I don't know what I'd do!"

The Counselor's Dilemma

Undoubtedly deciding what action you should take in a situation like this is a dilemma. Although it is required by law that all incidents of child abuse be reported, you ask yourself, "Is making this report worth risking the destruction of a family?" It is possible that Jonathon could be removed from his home. Furthermore, it is difficult to act on something that has been told you in confidence. But at the same time you know perfectly well that the abuse will almost certainly continue.

The ideal thing would be to persuade the abusive parent to seek help voluntarily. But this is not always possible. All fifty states now have laws requiring that incidents of child abuse be reported to the designated child-protection agency. In eighteen states, anyone knowing of or suspecting child abuse is required by law to report it. In other states, only certain professionals are required to report. If you are reluctant to identify yourself, all states provide anonymity and immunity from prosecution to anyone willing to report actual or suspected abuse.

In most cases of child abuse, either someone like us is told about the problem or evidence of the abuse is observed. Yet the situation is allowed to continue, sometimes until the child is killed. Why? Because neighbors and friends, teachers and ministers—people just like us—are hesitant to do or say anything. Many regard the family as sacrosanct, a sphere of life in which others have no right to interfere. That is why an estimated one-third to one-half of child abuse cases are never reported.

The decision whether to report an abusive but repentant parent like Jonathon's mother is indeed difficult. It may help to remember this: A child cannot be helped unless his or her plight is reported.

You explain to the distraught mother on the telephone that the first concern for her as well as for you is her little boy's well-being. You know that she is concerned, you say. You know that she realizes that there is a problem, otherwise she wouldn't have called you. Her call for help, you tell her, is not a sign of weakness. It is a sign of wisdom. You assure her that there are people who can and will help her.

"I don't know, . . ." she says hesitantly. "I feel a lot better after talking to you. I'm sure I can handle myself from now on."

You aren't so sure. In a kind but definite way you tell her that although you know she loves her son dearly and that she will do her best to control herself, you are concerned that she won't be able to do it. You tell her that quite honestly you are concerned about Jonathon's safety. When she doesn't respond, you tell her in as kind a way as you can that should she decline to seek help, you will have no choice but to inform the appropriate authorities.

"You're right," she finally says. "Who should I call?"

Where to Turn for Help

By being willing to accept help, Jonathon's mother is on her way to recovery. And help is available. Most communities have child-protection agencies and community mental health centers equipped to assist in cases of child abuse. Many also have local hotlines available to parents who feel they are losing control. The hotline counselors give them an opportunity to talk out their anger with a sympathetic listener. Even if there is no local hotline, there are national, toll-free numbers that are operated twenty-four hours a day.

Another possibility for help and support are the many therapy centers where parents and children can come together in a comfortable, neutral atmosphere and work out their tensions with the help of experienced advisers. In groups like Parents Anonymous, which is patterned after Alcoholics Anonymous, abusive parents can work to control their behavior through the support of their peers.

You make some referrals to Jonathon's mother and ask her to promise you that she will pursue them. She makes that promise. Even though her determination to get help seems completely sincere, you know that you will need to follow up with her. For Jonathon's sake, she must not change her mind.

For Jonathon's mother, change is possible. Change is possible for almost all abusive parents. The destructive cycle can be broken. But it cannot be done alone.

A QUICK OVERVIEW

Children beaten and abused by their own parents—the idea is shocking. Yet some experts believe that, given the right set of circumstances, it is possible for any parent to lose control and injure a child.

As crisis counselors, our first concern should be the safety of the child. Our next aim should be to persuade the abuser to seek help voluntarily. Remind the parent that rather than being a sign of weakness or immaturity, it is a sign of strength and wisdom.

If the abusive parent cannot or will not cooperate, we as crisis counselors must decide whether or not to report that abuse and the abuser to the proper authorities. As we make this decision we must remember that, regardless of promises and good intentions, the abuse is unlikely to stop unless the parent gets help. The physical and emotional well-being of the child is at stake.

Selecting which professionals and organizations we will use in referrals for an abusive parent is important. It is also important that we follow up to make sure that the family is in fact getting the help they need.

DOS AND DON'TS

Because child abuse is a potentially fatal situation, it must never be treated lightly. Whether the abuse has been mild or severe—or even if a parent is only fearful that it *will* happen—the matter must be taken seriously. Only a professional trained in this field is qualified to determine the seriousness of the problem and the right treatment for it.

Do ...

- Rethink your own position on the rights of parents. Understand that children are not pieces of property, but human beings. Their welfare must be carefully defended.
- Understand that most people truly want to be good parents. This is especially true of a parent who willingly seeks help.
- Affirm that it is not God's will that any child be raised with abusive or brutal discipline.
- Insist that the abuser accept the responsibility for her own behavior.
- Assure the abuser that her treatment of her child does not

47

mean that she is a bad mother. It does mean that she needs help in coping with this part of her life.

- Be gentle. Assure the abuser that she can learn to be the warm, loving parent she wants to be.
- Know what the reporting requirements are in your state.
- Remember that every state has laws requiring that incidents of child abuse be reported to a designated child-protection agency. That agency is qualified to determine the extent of the problem and to guide any treatment program.
- Cooperate with the local agencies that are charged with protecting abused children.
- Differentiate between a disciplining spank and true abuse.
- Emphasize the need for the abuser to get immediate, professional help.
- Assure her that help is available and that there is no disgrace in obtaining it.
- Learn to recognize the signs of abuse. The most common signs are repeated injuries or ones with questionable causes ("He's so careless, he's always falling down the stairs"); or tips from concerned friends, teachers, or relatives. We must not depend on an abuser's coming to us to reveal the problem. Often, if abuse is reported, the abuser will deny the charges.
- Understand that the problem does not disappear by itself. It not only continues, but usually worsens if left untreated.
- Refer only to agencies experienced in handling cases of child abuse or individuals well-qualified to counsel abusers.

Don't ...

- Act as a judge.
- Attempt to reassure the mother by explaining that it is natural for a mother to become irritated with her children. Irritation is natural, but acts of abuse are not.
- Tell her to settle down, "behave," and be a good mother.
- Tell her to control herself. She cannot do it.
- Give platitudes and simple advice. After you hear the story you may feel certain that a little helpful advice and common sense, a time of prayer and encouragement to seek God's help, are all that is needed. This is seldom the case.
- Be too quick to offer the abuser another chance. When there is a pattern of abuse, it will seldom stop without treatment.

- Deny that this problem exists in good Christian homes. It does.
- Refuse to get involved. Because many well-meaning but misguided people firmly believe that how a parent raises her child is no one else's business, child abuse is allowed to continue.
- Think that because a child doesn't tell, the abuse isn't happening.
- Ever agree to cover for a parent's abusive action.
- Confuse discipline with abuse. Never commend discipline that leaves welts and bruises on a child.
- Accept abusive discipline as God's will for raising a child.
- Try to diagnose whether or not the abuse is serious enough to require help. A wrong diagnosis could destroy a child emotionally and physically.
- Hold back from reporting abuse or suspected abuse because you have no solid proof or because you don't want to cause trouble. Nonabusing parents will not be held unjustly because of a complaint against them.
- Resist calling because you cannot give your name. If necessary, you can call anonymously.

When a woman comes to us with the accusation that her husband is abusing a child, we should suggest that she . . .

- Be sure that what is occurring is truly abuse. What one parent may interpret as abuse may merely be another's stricter discipline. If there is any doubt, the couple should discuss it with an experienced counselor they both respect.
- Understand that the abuse cannot continue without her consent. Being passive and doing nothing is the same as consenting to what her husband is doing.
- Steadfastly refuse to cover for his abusive acts. It is vital that the abuser be forced to accept the responsibility for his actions.
- Must take the child and leave unless she can induce him to seek help.

RESOURCES

The following national organizations exist to help parents and children:

National Child Abuse Hotline: 1–800–422–4453

Parents Anonymous. This organization has chapters in many communities throughout the United States. It also has a hotline that operates around the clock.

Hotline Number: 1–800–421–0353.
In California it is 1–800–352–0386.
In New York State it is 1–800–462–6406.

Parents United. Chapters of this volunteer self-help group have been established in many communities around the country.

Child Protection Division of the American Humane Association

Childhelp. This organization operates a twenty-four-hour hotline: 1–800–4–A–CHILD (1–800–422–4453).

National Center for Prevention of Child Abuse and Neglect

University of Colorado Medical Center
Denver, CO 80210
(303) 321–3963

National Coalition of Domestic Violence

1500 Massachusetts Ave.
Room 35
Washington, DC 20005

The National Committee for Prevention of Child Abuse

332 South Michigan Ave.
Chicago, IL 60604

Child Welfare League of America

SCAN (Stop Child Abuse Now). This organization has a number of chapters nationwide. Check the telephone directory to discover if there is a local chapter.

SUGGESTED READING

Fisher, Patricia Ann. *Gingerbread Girl.* Grand Rapids: Zondervan, 1985.

A tragic, true story of an abused child who found temporary protection in a loving foster home only to be further victimized by uncaring social workers, judges, and courts.

Hyde, Margaret O. *Cry Softly! The Story of Child Abuse.* Philadelphia: Westminster Press, 1980.

For children ages 12 to 14.

Quinn, P. E. *Cry Out! Inside the Terrifying World of an Abused Child.* Nashville: Abingdon Press, 1985.

A searing account of one child's abuse as told from the child's point of view, a story that is true and hopeful.

LOCAL REFERENCES

PARENTS ANONYMOUS

Number:

WELFARE DEPARTMENT

Number:

Contact Person:

SUPPORT GROUPS

These may include mothers' groups at church, YMCA, or YWCA.

NAME:

Number:

Contact Person:

Notes:

NAME:

Number:

Contact Person:

Notes:

NAME:

Number:

Contact Person:

Notes:

For other local organizations, hotlines, and private child abuse prevention services, look in the telephone directory for listings under the heading "Child Abuse."

NAME:

Number:

Contact Person:

Notes:

NAME:

Number:

Contact Person:

Notes:

HOW CAN THE CHRISTIAN COMMUNITY HELP?

Some sociologists believe that our society's changing lifestyles are at least partly to blame for the increase we are seeing in child abuse. People feel isolated and no longer can depend on the extended family to help them deal with problems.

Caring, dependable women and couples in the community who are willing to take a child for an hour or a day or longer when the child's parent needs a break can provide a truly valuable ministry. When compiling a list of such people, be sure to include specifics concerning time limitations, ages they would be willing to accept, and other pertinent information.

NAME:

Number:

Specifics:

NAME:

Number:

Specifics:

4. *Child Molestation*

Thomas was a pillar of the church. Although he was a hard-working family man, he always found the time to take on one more task. He had taught the first-grade Sunday school class for as long as anyone could remember. When the church needed a Junior Church, he started one. Some parents thought a church Boy Scout troop would be a good idea, and Thomas took that on, too. As in most churches, it was always hard to get enough Vacation Bible School teachers. Thomas normally worked during the day, but he gladly rearranged his work schedule so that he could help out. Sometimes he even took his vacation time to do it.

How the children loved Thomas! He was like a pied piper— wherever he happened to be, he was surrounded by a horde of his "little friends."

Just when you've decided there isn't a more wonderful Christian man anywhere than Thomas, Linda, another member of the church, comes to see you.

You and Linda have known each other for a long time. So why, you wonder, is she so ill at ease? Your attempts at small talk fail. It is obvious that she is terribly distressed.

"I have something to tell you," Linda says, "but I don't know how to start. My daughter, Robin, is just a little girl, you know. She's only five. I realize that kids have great imaginations and they make up lots of stuff. Maybe this is just something Robin made up. I really don't know. . . ."

You ask Linda what it was that her daughter told her.

"It's about Thomas," she says hesitantly. "Robin says he has done things to her."

You ask what kind of things.

"She says he likes to give her baths. Then he puts powder and lotion all over her. And I mean *all* over her. I can't believe the places she says he has touched her!"

You ask Linda when this happened.

"Well, Robin says he has done it a lot, but it was last night's experience that she finally told me about. Thomas was watching

Robin while I was out for the evening. I had already bathed her before I left, but she says he made her take off her nightgown and get in the tub again. She protested, but he told her if she didn't she would get a bad rash and I would be angry with both of them and wouldn't let him baby-sit for her anymore. You know Thomas better than I do. What do you think?"

You aren't sure what to think. Thomas surely doesn't look like a child molester. But then, what do molesters look like? We tend to think of them as dirty old men in raincoats who hang around playgrounds and schools offering candy to unsuspecting children. Some molesters fit this stereotype, but that is by no means the norm. A molester can be a doctor, a minister, a policeman, a teacher. He can be almost anyone. What separates child molesters from everyone else is not an external trait; it's what they do to children.

Furthermore, like Robin, about 80 percent of molestation victims know their attackers. Often they are family members or, like Thomas, trusted family friends.

"Do you think Robin was making this all up?" Linda asks.

You tell her that it is unlikely. It is important to believe children when they tell you about inappropriate sexual behavior directed toward them by an adult. According to experts children—especially the very young—seldom lie about such things.

All at once it strikes Linda that this thing she has feared, but had tried so hard to convince herself had not happened, is a fact. "Why my daughter?" she cries. "With all the kids in the country, with so many in this church, why did it have to be my Robin?"

It is easy to understand Linda's anger and frustration, but she doesn't realize the enormous extent of the problem of child molestation. Robin is by no means alone. Studies indicate that before they turn eighteen as many as half of all girls and 10 percent of all boys are sexually abused. Yet experts estimate that only one in ten incidents of child sexual abuse is ever reported. Furthermore, it is unlikely that Robin is Thomas's only victim, or even his only victim within the church. According to a study by the New York Psychiatric Institute's Sexual Behavior Clinic, the average molester has abused a total of seventy-three people!

"I feel like such a fool!" Linda exclaims. "I should have known there was something wrong when Thomas was so willing to baby-sit for Robin. He said his concern was for me, that being a single parent I needed a chance to get out. He seemed like such a good Christian man!"

You assure Linda that she has no reason to feel guilty. You tell her that you are just as surprised at Thomas's behavior as she is, that you never suspected that he might be a pedophile.

Signs to Raise Suspicions

By definition, pedophilia is a medical term used to describe adults who are attracted sexually to children. Some are women, but the vast majority—90 percent—are men and older boys. A pedophile is usually attracted to one sex, rarely to both. And he usually has a very specific age preference. The actions of pedophiles range from fondling or exhibitionism to long-term sexual affairs.

Although there is no easy way to identify a potential child molester, there are some signs that should raise suspicion:

- An adult who does not respect a child's request that he stop tickling, patting, or persisting in other physical contact
- An adult who "flirts" with children
- An adult with whom a child feels uncomfortable
- An adult or teenager who prefers the company of children rather than having friends his own age
- A loner who is not able to function socially with adults
- Someone who gives a child expensive gifts or money
- Someone who consistently entices children to his home

Sometimes, however, there are no clues. Because it is difficult to tell who is a potential molester, a parent should be especially careful and selective about anyone with whom she leaves her child alone.

"If this has been going on so long, why didn't Robin say something sooner?" Linda asks. "I mean, why would she let it continue? She's such a *good* little girl!"

Kids usually don't tell. Sometimes they fear that no one will believe them. Or they are afraid, especially if the molester has threatened them. Because of the abuser's warnings they may worry about what will happen to them ("Your parents will be mad at you and will send you away") or about what will happen to the abuser ("They will lock me away in jail").

Linda is right about Robin being a "good girl." Good children are a molester's favorite kind. That may, in fact, be part of the problem. "Show me an obedient child," said a convicted molester, "and I'll show you an easy victim." Children are vulnerable in part because they are taught to be polite and agreeable to adults and are discouraged from saying no.

Child molesters rarely use violence. In no way do they want unwilling victims. They want children who can be seduced, tricked, or blackmailed into a sexual relationship. Molesters use a selection process whereby the child least likely to say no is the one most likely to be chosen. They will almost always give up on any who resist. Unfortunately, there are many children who don't.

"Thomas has been so good to Robin," Linda tells you. "Since I'm a single parent I'm at work all day. When I get home I'm often too tired to spend the time with her that she wants and needs. With no brothers and sisters, I know she gets lonely. I actually welcomed the attention Thomas showered on her. He took her to the beach, to the zoo, to the playground, the ice-skating rink, and the amusement park. He took her out for hamburgers and ice cream cones. He was always there when she needed him. You know, Robin used to say that Thomas was her very best friend. Isn't that ironic?"

Not really. Like most experienced molesters, Thomas went to a great deal of time, trouble, and expense to win the love and affection of his victim. Many seek out children like Robin who are lonely for affection and companionship. They are willing to be the friend the child needs.

As the child becomes more comfortable with him, the man may try some tickling or wrestling, then some "innocent" fondling. Sometimes, as with Thomas and Robin, the molester stops there. Sometimes he doesn't.

According to experts, almost all pedophiles collect child pornography. By showing it to a child, the molester convinces the youngster that sexual activity is normal, even desirable. Pointing out the smiles on the children's faces, he says, "See what a good time these kids are having? They are beautiful, but you are more beautiful than any of them. Let's take some pictures of you." Although the child might normally refuse to take her clothes off for a picture-taking session, when she is confronted with the picture of others she can be persuaded much more easily. In most cases, if the child has been "trained" properly, the seducer eventually persuades her to disrobe.

The deeper the children get involved, the more trapped they feel and the harder it is to break out of the relationship. The pedophile warns the child to keep everything a secret because if anyone finds out they will both be in trouble. Many children who see the seducer as their friend don't want to lose that friendship or to get him into trouble. If nothing else works, the molester may threaten to hurt the child or her parents. This seldom fails to keep the child quiet.

58

Believing the Unbelievable

You ask Linda how she reacted when Robin told her what was happening. "Well, I couldn't believe it," she says. "I kept telling her she must be mistaken, that she must have been imagining things. But she was pretty specific in her description of what happened. I was shocked, embarrassed, and ashamed. I wasn't sure what to do or what to believe. That's why I decided to come to you."

You assure her that she did the right thing. How severely a child is affected by the molestation—whether it is exposure, fondling, or rape—depends largely on the parents' reaction. If the child's family is able to remain relatively calm and supportive, she is less likely to suffer deep trauma. But when the parents react hysterically or blame the child for what has happened, it only reinforces and increases their little one's fear and guilt.

Linda's shock was understandable. So was her initial reaction that Robin might be imagining things or exaggerating what had actually happened. Ironically, a child's imagination *is* commonly used to bolster the case of the molester. Psychologists say that though children do sometimes invent tales, it is uncommon for them to invent sexual abuse. To help determine the accuracy of accusations, professionals suggest listening for details that would not normally be within the child's sphere of knowledge.

Sometimes parents simply don't want to believe a child, especially if the accused is a relative or a family friend. They prefer to think that the child imagined or provoked the incident. And that, of course, is just what the abuser will say happened.

Why?

"Why is Thomas like that?" Linda asks. "I mean, he really seems to love children. What causes such a seemingly nice person to act that way toward innocent little ones?"

That is a difficult question to answer. No single reason stands out to explain why a person becomes a child molester. The possibilities range from a need to feel powerful and in control to traumatic childhood experiences, including sexual abuse. The cause is most likely a combination of factors.

Some suggest that the molestation of children is encouraged by our society. However, a spokesperson for the Canadian National Clearinghouse on Family Violence claims that the problem is worldwide. One thing is certain: Pedophiles do not consciously choose to be attracted to children.

A more relevant question is, why does he act on his impulses? Experts maintain that many people have some degree of sexual interest in children, but they never act on it. Those who do either don't recognize the strong taboo against child molestation or else cannot control themselves. Like Thomas, they purposely seek out positions that will put them in contact with children: scout leaders, coaches, workers in schools, camps, preschools, churches.

"Thomas didn't actually *hurt* Robin," Linda says tentatively. "Maybe it would be best just to warn him not to do anything like this again."

Where a child molester is concerned, a warning seldom means anything. Once he begins these activities he is driven to satisfy his needs at the expense of children. One study of arrest records and confessions tallied an average of seventy-three victims for each heterosexual pedophile and thirty for each homosexual child molester. The majority of molesters will never change.

When the molester is a well-liked man, an apparently "good" Christian, it is hard to report him. While you don't want him to hurt other children, you cannot bear the thought of his being locked up in jail or confined to a mental hospital. Thomas is someone you know. He's not a bad person.

Without a doubt, you are faced with a difficult decision. But keep in mind that it is not your responsibility to determine how "disturbed" the molester is. Leave that to the professionals. All things considered, you should report the offender to the authorities. Turning him in is not an act of revenge, nor is it judgment on your part. You are simply offering help to the violator and protection to his potential victims.

"What about Robin?" Linda asks you. "Will this have a permanent effect on her?"

Molesters do hurt children, sometimes physically and almost always in spirit. Children who fall victim to a molester—whether the act was fondling or rape—suffer from feelings of helplessness, shame, loneliness, guilt, and confusion. Many children survive sexual abuse with no apparent ill effects. This will probably be the case with Robin. But damage can be great if the victim has no suitably responsive adult with whom she can talk. Some victims may need professional counseling and therapy.

You have some referrals for Linda and suggestions of books that might be helpful, some for herself and some to read to Robin. She thanks you for your help and, after a time of prayer together, she leaves.

Alone in your office, you can't keep your mind off Thomas. It doesn't seem fair to report him to the authorities without first confronting him. You call him and ask him to stop by your office. He arrives within a half-hour.

It isn't easy to tell Thomas the charges that have been made against him. At first he denies everything. You tell him that you have no choice but to call the authorities. He argues and objects. When this fails, he begs you to let the matter drop.

As a counselor you realize that even if you wanted to, you couldn't let the matter drop. There is a great risk in confronting someone like Thomas, because making an accusation will trigger a detonation in the family like an atomic bomb. The fallout is tremendous. There is no turning back once you reach this point.

You ask him again if he did indeed give Robin baths. He said he did. "But there was nothing wrong with it," he insists. "She's just a little girl, for goodness sake! She needs to be bathed."

You ask about the powder and lotion. "It was just to protect her skin," he says. "If you ask me, you and Linda both have awfully dirty minds. I wouldn't hurt Robin. I wouldn't hurt *any* little child. I love children!"

Child molesters are very careful to cover their tracks and avoid discovery. If they are caught, they are almost certain to deny their actions. Should the proof be so convincing that they can no longer deny it, they try many ways to justify what they have done, often placing the blame on the child. Unless molesters come to the place where they will accept their guilt, little can be done to help them.

What to Do

Many professionals warn that even when molesters accept the responsibility for their actions, a cure is not likely. That is not to say that they shouldn't be treated, however; they certainly should be. But society must also be protected from repeat offenders.

So what should be done with offenders like Thomas? That's a good question. Judges often sentence them to probation with the requirement that they get therapy. The problem is that therapy isn't very effective in most cases. Even so, it usually doesn't take long for the offender to learn the right things to say to convince everyone that he no longer poses a threat so that he can quickly be released from the program. If they are sent to prison, child molesters—who are generally despised by the other inmates—are often beaten, raped, or

61

even murdered by their fellow prisoners. Furthermore, few prisons offer even a truly repentant molester any kind of therapeutic treatment.

What about the power of God? Can't He heal a child molester? We know He can. The problem is that a man such as Thomas is quick to claim a "healing," knowing that it is unlikely that the Christian community will question his sincerity. A violator who is truly willing to allow God to heal Him will first accept responsibility for what he has done. He will also be willing to cooperate with whatever treatment and therapy are ordered for him. Most of all he will prove his sincerity by staying away from temptation; he will voluntarily remove himself from contact with children. If he is not willing to do this, we have a right to question the validity of his "healing."

It has been charged that the church is especially susceptible to exploitation by abusers because volunteers are quickly welcomed into Sunday school and youth programs with little thought given to their backgrounds or possible motives. Too often young children are unquestioningly entrusted to anyone who is willing to work with them.

It would be wise for every church to provide training to parents and children on how to reduce the possibility of molestation. Luring children with money, food, gifts, or favors contributes to many cases of child molestation. The old admonition "Don't take candy from strangers" is still good advice, but only if the instruction goes much further than this. Children won't automatically connect an offer of candy with a risky situation. Some of the points that should be included are:

- Let children know that they have a right to say no.
- Never leave children alone with an adult about whom there is even the slightest reason for concern.
- Screen baby sitters carefully. If a child shows a dislike for a particular baby sitter, don't ask him or her back.
- Any adult who has only children for friends should be suspect. Normal people who like children also have healthy relationships with other adults.
- Keep the lines of communication with your own children open. Let them know that they can tell you anything.
- Set up a family rule that no secrets are to be kept except between children of the same age. ("Secrets" are different

from "surprises," which are pleasant things you eventually want to share.)

- Remind children that even "nice" people do bad or hurtful things.
- Urge children to tell about anyone who makes them feel uncomfortable. If a child feels uncomfortable with the hugs and kisses of a relative or friend, his parents should not encourage the child to put up with it.
- Prepare children to deal with bribes and threats as well as with possible physical force.
- Tell children that the parts of their bodies that are covered by a bathing suit are private, and if someone touches them there, or makes them touch him there, it is wrong and should be reported.
- Warn children never to go near a car with someone in it, and never to get into a car without their parents' permission.
- Instruct children to tell about money or gifts that are given to them no matter who it is who does the giving.
- Instruct children never to go into anyone's home without the knowledge and consent of their parents.
- Tell children that if a situation seems menacing, they should scream and run away.

Some adults fear that instruction such as this will frighten children. If it is handled well, it is not likely to do so. If the situation is not treated as something fearful, children will not be fearful.

A QUICK OVERVIEW

Child abusers are not all dirty old men who lurk around playgrounds offering candy to children. Most are kindly, respected men—a family friend or a relative of the victim. They can be found anywhere, even in church. Anytime a child makes an accusation of having been molested, the charge should be taken seriously; children seldom make up such stories.

Once he has started his sexually abusive behavior, the molester is unlikely to stop it on his own. Even with treatment the recovery rate is very low. For the protection of other children, it is important that the offender, no matter who he is, be reported to the proper authorities.

While most Christians agree that God can restore a child molester to full emotional health, merely the offender's assurance that this has happened should not be sufficient. An offender who is truly willing to seek God's healing will first admit and accept responsibility for what he has done. He will also be willing to cooperate with whatever treatment and therapy are ordered for him. Furthermore, a repentant molester should prove his sincerity by staying away from temptation—he will voluntarily remove himself from contact with children.

DOS AND DON'TS

Do ...

- Tell the parent to encourage the child to talk about what happened.
- Thoroughly investigate any statement regarding actual or attempted assault. No person should be considered above suspicion.
- Emphasize that the child is not to blame.
- Tell the parent the importance of offering the child support and understanding. Encourage her to guard against over-reacting to the point of frightening the child even more than the incident itself did.
- Strongly encourage the parent to report the incident to the police or child welfare authorities. Even if it is only a suspicion, it should be reported. It will be kept confidential until the facts are known.
- Report the molestation on your own if the parent refuses to do so.
- Warn the parent to be sure that a social worker or someone supportive to the child is present when the evidence is given.
- Instruct the parent not to "correct" the child's story. If the police want to talk with the child, the officer will want to hear the original account, even if it includes babyish or family words. If another person tries to suggest or modify what the child is trying to say, those ideas might confuse the truth.
- Warn the parent against making angry threats about what will happen to the offender. This might cause the child to feel guilty about telling. A better statement would be, "What Thomas did was wrong. We're going to see that he gets help so that he doesn't hurt you or anyone else again."
- Remind the parent to respect the child's privacy. The abuse should be discussed only with trusted friends and never in front of the child.

- Tell the parent to determine whether or not the child has been injured physically. If so, she should seek medical care immediately. The doctor's report might be especially important if the case should later come to trial.
- Encourage the entire family to seek professional counseling if there is a possibility of emotional damage.

Don't ...

- Show horror, shock, or disgust at anything you are told. Such a reaction will make it even more difficult for the parent or child to continue an account that is very hard to discuss anyway.
- Even hint that the parents were negligent or foolish in permitting this to happen. Even if you think so, there is no reason to heighten their sense of guilt.
- Assume that if the molestation went no further than exhibition or touching, the incident isn't important.
- Believe that the experience is not traumatic to the child. Even if it did not involve physical contact, it can be damaging emotionally.
- Think that the damage can be undone simply by having the offender apologize.
- Believe a particular person is incapable of such actions.
- Be afraid or too embarrassed to use explicit language when necessary. As one psychologist has stated, "It's hard to take the sex out of sexual abuse."
- Be hesitant to take the word of a young child. Remember, children seldom make up or exaggerate stories with sexual connections.
- Allow yourself to be swayed by what the accused molester might tell you. He may be telling you the truth, but it is also possible that he is not. Molesters are usually experts at manipulation.

RESOURCES

The following organizations can offer further information on the subject of sexual molestation of children:

Child Protection Center

Children's Hospital
111 Michigan Avenue, N.W.
Washington, DC 20010

National Coalition Against Sexual Assault (NCASA). For material on how to protect children from sexual abuse, contact the office nearest you.

Northeast: Albany County Rape Crisis Center
112 State Street
Room 640
Albany, NY 12207

Southeast: 5495 Murray Street
Memphis, TN 38119

Midwest: Loop YWCA/Women's Services
37 South Wabash Avenue
Chicago, IL 60603

South: National Office
Austin Rape Crisis Center
P.O. Box 7156
Austin, TX 78713

West: 416 South 25 Street
Laramie, WY 82070

Farwest: Office of Criminal Justice Planning
9719 Lincoln Village Drive
Sacramento, CA 95827

National Committee for Prevention of Child Abuse. For two dollars this group will send a packet containing a listing of books, films, and programs on the prevention of sexual abuse.

Sexual Abuse Prevention Material
Box 2866
Chicago, IL 60690

Parents United

P.O. Box 952
San Jose, CA 95108

Sexual Assault Center

Harborview
325 9th Avenue
Seattle, WA 98104

Society's League Against Molestation (SLAM). This group is dedicated to creating public awareness about child molestation and now has more than seventy-five chapters in forty-three states. More information is available by writing, enclosing a self-addressed, stamped envelope to:

524 South First Avenue
Arcadia, CA 91006

SUGGESTED READING

Adams, Caren, and Jennifer Fay, *No More Secrets: Protecting Your Child From Sexual Abuse.* San Luis Obispo: Impact Publishers, 1981.

Edwards, Katherine. *A House Divided.* Grand Rapids: Zondervan, 1984.

Fortune, Marie M. *Sexual Violence: The Unmentionable Sin.* New York: Pilgrim, 1983.

> Written by a Protestant minister who has worked for several years with the Center for the Prevention of Sexual and Domestic Violence. Practical strategies for Christian ministers dealing with several types of abusers and their victims.

Hyde, Margaret O. *Sexual Abuse: Let's Talk About It.* Philadelphia: Westminster Press, 1984.

> Tells young people and those concerned about them how to prevent sexual abuse. Includes actual case histories and examples, suggested further readings, and a list by state of concerned organizations. For ages 10 and older.

It's My Body and accompanying Parents Resource Guide. Everett, Wash.: Planned Parenthood of Snohomish County.

> Recommended for children 3 to 8 years old. Address: 2730 Hoyt Ave., Everett, WA 98201.

Joyce, Irma. *Never Talk to Strangers.* Racine, Wis.: Western Publishing, Gold Books.

Rush, F. *The Best Kept Secret: Sex Abuse of Children.* Englewood Cliffs, N.J.: Prentice-Hall, 1980.

Sgroi, Suzanne M. *Handbook of Clinical Intervention in Child Sexual Abuse.* Lexington, Mass.: D. C. Heath, Lexington Books, 1983.

Stowell, Jo, and Mary Dietzel. *My Very Own Book About Me.* Spokane: Lutheran Social Services of Washington.

> Address: N. 1226 Howard, Spokane, WA 99201.

Wachter, Oralee. *No More Secrets for Me*. Boston: Little, Brown, 1983.

> For ages 4 to 12. Short stories to help children become aware of abusive situations and what to do if they are ever molested.

Also available:

Child Sexual Abuse Prevention: Tips for Parents.

> Send request to NCCAN Clearinghouse, P.O. Box 1182, Washington, DC 20013.

LOCAL REFERENCES

RAPE HOTLINE

Check your local telephone directory or request the number from the police department.

Number:

Notes:

PSYCHIATRIST, PSYCHOLOGIST, OR FAMILY COUNSELOR
NAME:

Number:

Notes:

NAME:

Number:

Notes:

MEDICAL DOCTOR
NAME:

Number:

Notes:

CHILD PROTECTION AGENCY

Number:

Contact Person:

Notes:

OTHER PEOPLE AND ORGANIZATIONS

These people and organizations may be helpful to children, families, or abusers.

NAME:

Number:

Notes:

NAME:

Number:

Notes:

5.   *Incest*

It's past nine o'clock in the evening when fifteen-year-old Shelley appears at your door. "I've run away from home," she informs you. "And I won't ever go back! No one can make me go back!"

You attempt to talk to her, to reason with her. You assure her of her parents' love and tell her that they are certain to be very concerned about her. But when you say that you have no choice but to call her parents and tell them where she is, she suddenly breaks down and tells you why she has run away. For the past five years, Shelley says, she has been a victim of incest. The molester is her father.

The problem of incest has long been ignored as an abhorrent but mercifully rare occurrence. Abhorrent it is. Rare it is not. While fifteen years ago experts were claiming that incest occurred in no more than one family in a million, some now believe that one in a hundred is a more realistic figure.

Broadly defined, incest includes any sexually arousing physical contact between unmarried family members so closely related that they are forbidden by law to marry. The precise legal definition, as well as the punishment associated with it, varies from state to state.

Like other crimes committed against family members, incest frequently goes unreported. The violation of the taboo against it is so repellent that the offender and the victim, and often other family members who discover the relationship as well, go to extraordinary lengths to hide it. The silence has served to protect the offender and to deny help to the victim.

Still, you find Shelley's charges awfully hard to believe. You know her father. He is a good man—a Boy Scout leader, a deacon in the church, and a respected member of the community. Could Shelley be fabricating this terrible story for some reason? It's not likely. As with the victims of other types of molestation, children almost never lie about such an experience.

It is much more comfortable to think of incestuous adults as dangerous criminals or deranged psychotics, but the truth is that this is seldom the case. More often he is an otherwise law-abiding, regular, man-next-door type of guy who somewhere along the line lost the ability to control his impulses.

It has been said that many people who commit incest are simply child molesters who stay home. In fact, statistics indicate that 34 percent of the cases of sexual abuse of children take place in the victim's own home. Because incest is a type of child molestation, much of what was said in the preceding chapter applies here.

The Classic Pattern

Shelley and her father fit the classic picture of an incestuous relationship. Girls are victims more often than boys. The offender is usually the father or stepfather. The relationship usually begins when a girl is under twelve years of age, for that is when she is most easily controlled. Physical force is seldom necessary. Most incestuous relationships last at least a year, often much longer. The majority of victims are warned never to tell what is going on, and most of them obey.

Although father/stepfather-daughter incest is the type most frequently reported, it is by no means the only sexual abuse that occurs within families. Brothers, sisters, uncles, aunts, grandparents, and cousins have been known to be involved. So have mothers, although this is much less common.

"I love my dad," Shelley insists through her tears. "And I'm sure he loves me, too. Except for this one thing, he's always been very good to me. I don't want to get him into trouble, but I hate what he's doing to me. I just can't stand it anymore!"

You ask Shelley if her father ever used force on her. She says no. "I trusted him," she says. "He said what we were doing was all right, so I just believed him."

Because a daughter naturally trusts her father, she usually reacts exactly as Shelley did. But because she has put up no struggle, the victim often ends up believing that she has participated in the act voluntarily. This causes her to feel responsible for doing something wrong and compounds her feelings of guilt. It also supports the abuser's claim that "she liked it."

You listen to everything Shelley has to say, letting her know that you believe what she is telling you. You assure her that she has done the right thing by coming to you, that in no way has she betrayed her father. You explain that her father's actions were very wrong; that he, the adult, was responsible for what happened, not her.

You ask Shelley if her mother is aware of what has been going on. She says no. You tell her that incest is a crime, that you have no choice but to report this to the police. You tell her that her mother will have to know about it and suggest that she be called right away. Shelley tearfully agrees.

When her mother arrives, Shelley is curled up in a corner of the couch, her face hidden. The mother's first words to her daughter are, "How could you have let this happen, Shelley? You aren't a child! You could have stopped it!"

It often happens in cases of sexual abuse that the victim herself is forced to bear the most blame. This is especially likely to occur when, to all appearances, the victim is more woman than child. It's difficult to accept the fact that Shelley is as much an innocent victim as a three-year-old youngster. But the truth is that at any age a child generally accepts the abuse and learns to live with it simply because she thinks she has no choice.

"You always taught me to trust my dad and to obey him," Shelley says softly. "I just didn't know how to make him stop."

Shelley will almost certainly need professional counseling and therapy to overcome the wounds that have been systematically inflicted on her by her father. Without this help she will pay a high price for the abuse she has suffered at the hands of a person she loved and trusted. Because her first experiment with trust was such a painful failure, she will not easily trust again. This means that she will very likely have trouble developing satisfying relationships with other people. Like many incest victims, she may confuse love, guilt, and sex.

"Why didn't you tell me?" her mother demands.

"Dad made me promise not to tell anyone. He said no one would understand. He said I'd be badly punished and he'd be put in jail. I remember thinking that if he was locked up, you would have to go to work and there would be no one to take care of me and the little kids."

Secrecy is a necessary ingredient in virtually all cases of child molestation. Often incest involves all the daughters in a family, each one keeping the secret and thinking that she is protecting the others from the reality of what is happening. They all suffer, but each one suffers alone. As with Shelley, the fear that the awful secret could destroy the family keeps many children quiet.

Shelley's mother starts to ask another question, but you interrupt. You know that a child or young person who is believed and receives emotional support has a much better chance of recovering from her devastating experiences. What Shelley needs now from her mother is emotional support, not accusation.

Breaking the Secrecy

You remind the mother that you are required by law to report incidents of incest.

"Please don't call the police," Shelley's mother pleads. "There is no reason to get them involved. I'll have Shelley stay with her aunt for a week or two until this blows over and I have a chance to work this out with my husband."

You tell her that you can't make such an agreement with her. For healing to be possible for either Shelley or her father, the secrecy must be broken no matter how much it hurts.

If you are unsure how to proceed, get some telephone counseling. In most areas there is a child-abuse hotline. Many times the caller can talk directly to a social worker, who will advise what specific steps should be taken. The counselor can also explain what will happen to the offender, the victim, and the family as a whole if the situation is reported, and the dangers of not reporting it.

You make the necessary calls. The three of you wait for the social workers to arrive. When they come, Shelley and her mother leave with them. You say goodby and assure Shelley of your support and willingness to help in whatever way you can.

Less than two hours later there is another knock at your door. It's Ed, Shelley's father.

"My wife called me," he says. "I'm going to be arrested."

You ask him in. A tall, good-looking man in his mid-thirties, quiet spoken, and a respected church member, you find it difficult to believe that Ed is guilty of the terrible deeds of which his daughter has accused him. But with tears streaming down his face, Ed admits everything.

"Five years ago I lost my job," he says. "It was the most shattering experience of my life! My wife had to go to work to support the family. Because it was the only opening available, she took the three to midnight shift. I became a 'house husband,' and Shelley was my right-hand helper. Although she was only ten, she seemed to understand the problem our family was facing. She took on the care of the younger children, who were then three and five, and seemed to grow overnight from a little child to a responsible adult.

"Every night, after the little ones were in bed, Shelley would make hot cocoa for the two of us, then she would snuggle up by me on the couch and we'd watch television together, just like my wife and I used to do before she went back to work. It was the most pleasant time of the day—just me and the girl who thought I was the greatest guy in the world. Somehow things escalated from there. More and more Shelley took on the role of my wife—first with the kids, then in the kitchen, then in my bed."

A Troubled Family

According to many professionals, incestuous fathers generally fall into four categories. The first is the natural father who is sexual with his young children. He is likely to be psychotic. The second is the one who takes advantage of his older kids. He is likely to see his child as taking the place of his wife. The third is the stepfather who molests younger stepchildren. Most likely he is a pedophile who has molested other kids and probably married his wife because of her children. The fourth is the stepfather who sexually abuses the teenagers of the family. This type of man often has a history of criminal or other antisocial behavior.

Of course, these categories are not rigid. It is sometimes difficult to determine just where an incestuous person falls in that assortment. But determining the root cause or the degree of guilt involved is not our function in counseling. No matter how well we might know the person involved, it is too easy to make a mistake. Leave the diagnosis to the professionals.

One factor that is almost universal with incestuous adults is a troubled family. Incest generally doesn't cause a family breakdown; it is the result of one. In families where incest occurs, there is usually little communication between family members, a lack of normal affection, and little mutual support. Also, an incestuous relationship often arises from the offender's feelings of inadequacy or loneliness, a desperate need for tenderness and understanding that his spouse fails to give him. The reasons for the behavior are more emotional than sexual.

It should be noted, however, that even a father who is responding to great emotional needs is guilty nonetheless and must bear responsibility for his behavior. There is no way to skirt the fact that at some point he made a conscious decision to act on his incestuous impulses.

"I knew what I was doing was wrong," Ed conceded. "At times I was so consumed with guilt that I considered killing myself. But I just couldn't bring myself to do that. Although I hated myself for what I was doing to my daughter, I couldn't stop.

"I know you will find this hard to understand, but I was able to come up with a thousand reasons to convince myself that what I was doing was okay, that I was different from those creeps and deviates who prowl the streets and alleys molesting children."

It has been noted that many fathers in incestuous relationships are religious men and regular church attenders. Some distort biblical passages to justify what they are doing. If that doesn't work, they point out passages to their daughters to show that they should "forgive and forget."

Because they cannot control themselves, religious men tend to rely on their beliefs to restrain them. Then, when they repeat their behavior, they blame the devil for making them do it or they blame God for not preventing it. Either way, it's not their fault. Incestuous adults, religious or not, are masters at evading responsibility for their actions.

"The problem is, my wife wasn't there when I needed her!" Ed states. "The only one who was there for me was Shelley."

Because his actions are rarely malicious, the aggressor often finds it fairly easy to maintain an air of innocence. Feeling misunderstood, he denies responsibility for his actions—even when, like Shelley's father, he admits what he has done—and instead places the blame on someone else. But the fact is that no combination of factors *has* to result in an act of incest. When it does, there is always an adult involved who has chosen to initiate the relationship. It must be understood that the responsibility for incest falls totally and directly on the adult.

Hope for Restoration

"I can't believe that our family has come to this," Ed says, shaking his head in despair. "What will happen to Shelley? What will happen to me? Is there any hope for our family?"

The answer is yes, there is hope. There is always hope. Even in the darkest of situations, God has the power to fully heal and totally restore. Because denial remains the greatest barrier to rehabilitation, Ed in admitting the problem has already taken a major step in the right direction.

Incest carries criminal penalties in all fifty states. In most it is a crime punishable by imprisonment, with penalties ranging from ninety days to a life sentence, although offenders are often given probation. Sometimes, especially when the offender pleads guilty, court-ordered therapy for the entire family is a condition of probation. Sometimes the children are removed from the home and placed in foster care, at least temporarily. At other times the offender is ordered to leave the home while he receives outpatient therapy.

Treatment programs developed in recent years have had a much better success rate for incest offenders than they have for child molesters in general. The good news is, numerous studies show that convicted incest offenders have one of the lowest rates of recurrence of all categories of crime. The bad news is, too many men steadfastly refuse to cooperate with therapists because they don't think there is anything wrong with them.

As with other types of domestic violence, the authorities usually set a priority on helping families end the abuse so that they can remain together. And, according to records, the majority of the families affected are eventually reunited. This is fine if the father is willing to face realistically what he has done and to cooperate with counselors, but this is not always the case. If the father won't cooperate, it often comes down to the mother being forced to choose between him and her daughter. Faced with such a decision, many women will choose to have the father remain at home and the victimized girl placed in foster care. When this happens, other girls in the family will very likely fall victim to their father also. After all, if the incest has borne him no real consequences, there is no reason to change.

And what about the victims? Those deprived of therapy and emotional support often grow up with many problems: low self-esteem, feelings of isolation, headaches and other physical ailments, depression that can lead to suicide, promiscuity, and crippling guilt.

Yet it is possible to survive the pain of incest, to have a happy life with rewarding, nonexploitive relationships, to feel safe and good about oneself again. In the final analysis, incest means that the entire family needs help. Ideally this help includes individual therapy and support groups for all members of the family.

The police arrive. With a sigh Ed says, "You know, I'm really glad Shelley came to you. I couldn't stop what I was doing. It would have continued until she left home. I'm glad it's finally over."

A QUICK OVERVIEW

Incest occurs much more frequently than most people think. It can happen in some very unlikely families, so it is important to believe any charges of sexual abuse.

Because it is an extension of child molestation, many of the same principles in the last chapters apply to incest. One great difference is that the prognosis for an incestuous adult is much better than it is for other kinds of child molesters.

There are different types of incestuous parents. Some can respond more favorably to therapy than others. Whatever their situation, they cannot be helped until they are willing to admit what has happened, to assume the responsibility for it, and to cooperate with therapy. Unless the victim receives professional help, she is certain to suffer permanent emotional scars.

DOS AND DON'TS

Because victims of incest are most likely to report their situation to a Sunday school teacher, pastor, youth leader, or someone else in a position of leadership, it is vitally important that we not only have some understanding of the problem, but also know how to respond in a positive, helpful way.

Incest is a type of child molestation, so much of the information in chapter 4 also applies here.

Do ...

- Encourage parents to believe their children when they report sexual abuse within the family. Children seldom invent such stories.
- Understand that incest is *never* the child's fault. It is up to the adult to refrain from taking advantage of the child.
- Assure the child that she did the right thing in telling what happened. Assure her that it is not wrong to break a promise to keep such a secret.
- Report any suspected case of incest. All reports are carefully checked out by professionals. If there is a mistake, the family will not be caused trouble or embarrassment. It is better to err on the side of caution than to allow a child to continue to be victimized.
- Emphasize to those involved that children are not the

78

property of their parents. Children have the right to grow up in an atmosphere free of abuse.

- Understand the spiritual ramifications of incest involving a Christian father. The victim's feelings about God's love and the reality of faith can be shattered by what she has experienced. ⸱
- Try to repair the damage done to the abused child's perception of God. Because our understanding of God comes in part from our fathers, you can imagine the spiritual problems faced by a child who has suffered incest at the hands of her father.
- Encourage the entire family to get counseling from an experienced, trained professional.
- Offer support to the entire family through this most difficult of experiences.
- Build trust in the victim by providing opportunities for her to be surrounded by trustworthy people.
- Try to develop a support network of Christians on whom family members can call when they need emotional support and an understanding ear.
- Believe, and reaffirm to those involved, that God has the power to heal the victim, the offender, and the entire family.

Don't ...

- Be fooled into thinking that incest is the result of too much family love. It is far more likely to occur in homes where children are hungry for affection.
- Think that incest cannot happen in "good Christian families." It can and it does.
- Ever disregard a charge of incest, no matter how hard it is for you to believe.
- Attempt to comfort the victim or her family with nice-sounding platitudes. This gives the impression that the whole thing is not all that important in your opinion.
- Put yourself in the position of psychiatrist. It is not our job to diagnose the underlying cause of the incestuous behavior of the adult. Nor should we try to determine the degree of damage that has been done to the child.
- Give the impression that if the abuse only happened a time or two, or if it never went beyond the fondling stage, it isn't a real problem. It is.

- Pass the incident off by saying that the victim is young and will forget all about it.
- Allow the offender to be dismissed with a promise to change. We cannot assume an incestuous relationship will stop without intervention.
- Blame other members of the family for "letting" this happen. By asking, "Why didn't you stop it?" we intensify the feelings of guilt that already plague them.

RESOURCES

More information on the subject of incest is available from the following organizations:

Austin Child Guidance Center

612 West 6th Street
Austin, TX 78701

Child Assault Prevention Project (CAP). National office:

Women Against Rape
P.O. Box 02084
Columbus, OH 43202

Child Protection Center

Children's Hospital
111 Michigan Avenue, N.W.
Washington, DC 20010

National Committee for Prevention of Child Abuse. A packet containing a list of books, films, and programs on the prevention of sexual abuse is available for two dollars from this organization. The address:

Box 2866
Chicago, IL 60690

Parents United/Daughters and Sons United. For information on local chapters of these helpful groups, write to them at this address:

P.O. Box 952
San Jose, CA 95108

Sexual Assault Center

Harborview
325 9th Avenue
Seattle, WA 98104

The following organizations provide help for the victim of incest:

V.O.I.C.E. (Victims of Incest Can Emerge)

Grand Junction, CO 81501
(303) 241–2746

Child Help USA

Woodland Hills, CA 91370
1–800–4–A–CHILD

Child Sexual Abuse Treatment Program

467 South Third Street
San Jose, CA 95110
(408) 299–2511

National Center for the Prevention of Child Abuse and Neglect

P.O. Box 1182
Washington, DC 20013
(202) 245–2856

Parents United/Daughters and Sons United. An address for these groups is given in the preceding section.

Counseling number: (408) 280–5055

SUGGESTED READING

Armstrong, Louise. *Kiss Daddy Goodnight*. New York: Hawthorn Books, 1978.
Bass, E., and Thornton L. Bass, editors, *I Never Told Anyone: Writings by Women Survivors*. New York: Harper & Row, 1983.
Edwards, Katherine. *A House Divided*. Grand Rapids: Zondervan, 1985.

The autobiography of an incest victim who is a former missionary. Also contains information on how to report incest, and lists agencies for legal, financial, and emotional aid.

Fortune, Marie. *Sexual Violence: The Unmentionable Sin*. New York: Pilgrim, 1983.
Forward, Dr. Susan, and Craig Buck. *Betrayal of Innocence*. New York: Penguin, 1979.

Hyde, Margaret O. *Sexual Abuse, Let's Talk About It*, Philadelphia: Westminster, 1985.

> Includes a list by state of concerned organizations. For ages 10 and older.

LOCAL REFERENCES

PARENTS UNITED

Call (408) 280–5055 for the local number or consult the telephone directory.

Number:

Contact Person:

DAUGHTERS AND SONS UNITED

See Parents United.

LOCAL MENTAL HEALTH AGENCY

Number:

Contact Person:

Notes:

PROFESSIONAL COUNSELOR

Choose one trained to work with incest victims.

NAME:

Number:

Notes:

82

NAME:

Number:

Notes:

LOCAL RAPE HOTLINE

Number:

Notes:

LOCAL SUPPORT GROUPS

NAME:

Number:

Notes:

NAME:

Number:

Notes:

NAME:

Number:

Notes:

OTHER HELPFUL PEOPLE OR AGENCIES

NAME:

Number:

Notes:

NAME:

Number:

Notes:

6. *Infidelity*

Sue makes a strained effort to hold back her tears. Her face ashen, she sits slumped in the chair and nervously twists her handkerchief.

"Maybe I shouldn't have come," she begins. "There's really nothing you can do. But I just had to talk to someone. I never thought I'd admit it, but I think I've finally encountered a problem that's too big for me to handle."

The problem Sue has come to talk about is infidelity. For several months her middle-aged, respected, churchgoing husband has been having an affair with a saleswoman from his office.

"I never thought this could happen to us," Sue tells you. "But it has. Jerry told me all about it last night.

"He says he still loves me and wants to stay with me and the children. And he assures me that it is all over between him and the woman at work and that nothing like this will ever happen again. He says he wants me to forgive him so that we can rebuild our marriage and everything can be like it was before. But I don't think that's possible. How can our relationship ever again be based on trust?"

How indeed? Unfaithfulness is the ultimate break of marriage trust, a total revoking of the sacred wedding vows made in the presence of God.

You ask Sue how she feels right now.

"I'm in shock," she answers. "I wish I could hate Jerry, but the truth is that he is a good man and a good father. And he used to be a good husband. Despite this mess, I still love him."

Sue probably thinks that she is the first person to come to you with the problem of infidelity. She's not. Just last week Joanne, a talented soprano soloist, sat in the same chair and told you about her ongoing affair with Charlie, another choir member.

Joanne's situation is different from Sue's. "I love my husband and I love my family," Joanne had told you. "I don't want to lose them, but to be perfectly honest, I'm not at all sure I can give Charlie up. It may sound impossible to you, but I am in love with both of them."

According to Joanne, the affair had started innocently enough. "Charlie and I were just good friends," she told you. "After choir practice we used to go out for coffee to unwind and talk. At first others went along, but we soon found that we enjoyed it more with just the two of us. We had a lot in common, including a need to communicate on an adult level with someone who was genuinely interested in what we had to say. My husband was too busy with his own concerns to listen to mine, and Charlie's wife, with three children under six, was worn out and ready for bed the minute she got the kids down.

"Those after-choir coffee hours were so pleasant that Charlie and I started extending them to luncheons. As time went on, we shared more and more intimate details of our lives. One thing led to another, and then one day there we were in my bed.

"I know you probably think we have committed a horrible sin. But it was, after all, God who put the love for each other into our hearts. I just know He understands. You can't imagine what a deep, caring relationship Charlie and I have. We never intended it to go so far, but now that it has, I just don't think we can ever go back."

Marriages in Trouble

Infidelity has become commonplace in our society. Extramarital affairs are portrayed on television and in the movies as an everyday thing. As such behavior becomes more and more accepted, Christians become increasingly tolerant of and vulnerable to it. In time, many, like Joanne, begin to see infidelity not so much as sin as "just one of those things that happen."

Professionals maintain that adultery occurs most often by far in marriages that are already in trouble. Infidelity intrudes when one partner attempts to fill a need that is missing in the marriage by finding an intimate relationship with someone else. Couples who openly face their difficulties before they get out of control are seldom faced with this problem.

Joanne would have you believe that the affair in which she is engaged is not really her fault. Because her husband isn't there to listen to her when she needs to talk, he is to blame. She even suggests that God is somehow at fault because He "put the love in our hearts." But the fact that there were problems in her marriage in no way relieves Joanne of the responsibility for her actions.

By the same token, you can comfort Sue by assuring her that she is not responsible for her husband's involvement with the woman at work. If her husband felt that there were problems in their marriage, he had a responsibility to discuss the matter with his wife so that together they could prayerfully work out the difficulties.

Where extramarital affairs are concerned, a double standard definitely exists. It is true that there seems to be more sexual infidelity among husbands than wives. But it is also true that our society's tolerance toward adulterous husbands is much greater than toward adulterous wives. This attitude is demonstrated in a survey conducted by Dr. Donald Granvold, a professor at the University of Texas at Arlington. Of the 262 marriage counselors questioned, 22 percent thought that marriages are jeopardized when the wife has an affair, while only 2 percent thought marriages are in trouble when the husband is the offender.

Had you been asked to respond to Dr. Granvold's survey, what would you have said? More important, how will you react to Sue and Joanne? Do you consider Joanne's sin greater than that of Sue's husband?

Regardless of which spouse strays, one thing is certain: Unfaithfulness in a marriage relationship is one of the most devastating experiences a man or woman can suffer. And although infidelity affects men and women differently—both in the reasons they become involved in such affairs and in the way they deal with the discovery of an adulterous spouse—marriage counselors have found that many emotions and concerns are the same.

Dealing With Pain and Rejection

When infidelity is occurring, a marriage relationship inevitably deteriorates. The problems that already exist are compounded. Any trust that might have managed to survive the previous difficulties is now destroyed by the deception that is taking place. And just imagine the severe blow a person's self-esteem suffers when he or she suddenly discovers that the spouse who has promised to love and cherish "till death do us part" has actually found a new sexual partner. The intensity of this rejection is like no other emotional distress a person can inflict on a spouse.

Joanne would have you believe that her infidelity is somehow overlooked by God. It is not. Adultery is *always* a sin, and sin *always* displeases God. Furthermore, sin inevitably leads to pain and suffering.

Sue knows something of the pain that comes from adultery. "After my husband told me about his affair he said, 'I'm glad it's out in the open. I feel so much better. It's like the weight of the world is off my back.' Well, I'm glad *he* felt better because *I* certainly didn't. I sat up all night and cried. It's as if a tidal wave of pain and hurt had swept me off my feet and was threatening to drown me.

"At times I was so overcome by anger that all I could think of was destroying him. Then the anger would be replaced by shame and humiliation. Then I would be consumed by guilt: What had I done that displeased Jerry so much that he was driven to seek out another woman? And then the incredible pain would wash over me again and I'd cry out, 'How could he do this to me? How could he break the trust, the promise he made to me before God?'

"Several times I had an overpowering desire to unleash all my anger and pain and do something cruel, something like smash his collection of antique model airplanes. I knew how much they meant to him, how many painstaking hours he had spent working on them, and I wanted so badly to hurt him. If I stomped those airplanes into a million pieces, maybe then he would have some idea of how I felt standing in the wreckage of my shattered marriage."

The feelings of extreme pain and rejection are heightened by the break with church friends that often occurs during adultery.

"I don't see them much any more," Joanne says of her Christian friends. "I guess my life is just too busy to find the time to get together with them. Anyway, we really don't seem to have that much in common now."

Carrying on an affair and trying to keep up some semblance of a home life would cut into Joanne's available time. But undoubtedly there are deeper reasons for her break with her Christian friends. Despite her insistence that she is not really doing anything "that wrong," she must be feeling some sense of guilt. Even if her friends were totally unaware of what was going on, this would likely cause her to feel uncomfortable with them. And it's certainly easier to deny the sinfulness of her actions when she keeps away from others who might challenge her rationalizing.

"I know what Christ said about the woman caught in adultery," Sue tells you. "He said, 'Let him who is without sin cast the first stone.' God knows *I'm* not without sin—far from it! I suppose the Christian thing for me to do would be to 'turn the other cheek.' If Jerry's running around was caused by something I did, or something I didn't do, I guess I should ask him what it was and try to change."

Joanne admitted that she isn't ready to break off her affair. She wanted her husband and family, but she also wanted Charlie. "My husband just needs to be patient with me while I work through my feelings," she reasoned. "It took a long time for our marriage to deteriorate to where I needed someone else, and it will take time to build it back up again. My husband should understand that. He could help me by reaffirming his love for me and making me feel special and cared for."

Difficult Choices

Joanne seems to be asking too much from her husband, Sue too little from hers. What is the proper response for a Christian who has an unfaithful spouse? Is that person to refrain from judging, to "turn the other cheek"? Is it better to pretend not to know and patiently concentrate on making such a happy home that the unfaithful partner will be irresistibly drawn back? Is it better to confront that person with the sinfulness of what he is doing? Or is it best to throw the adulterous spouse out, demand a divorce, and have it over with?

The choice between adopting a seemingly loving, nonjudgmental attitude and demanding accountability is a difficult one indeed. What Sue is considering seems to be a commendable Christian attitude. And in some cases this may be the right thing to do. Her husband does seem to be genuinely sorry for what he has done and determined to renew his commitment to her and to their marriage. On the other hand, her unconditional acceptance of the situation may be a signal to him that the whole matter is not really of that great concern to her. He may never realize the pain and anguish she has suffered because of his actions.

And how about Joanne's husband? As a Christian who is dedicated to his marriage, should he accept her terms? In many cases, especially when the unfaithful partner has no intention of committing herself to a faithful marriage, it is preferable for the spouse to insist on strict rules and specifications as a condition of continuing with the marriage.

It must be made clear to erring partners that they have to choose between their families and their adulterous behavior. They cannot have it both ways. What would happen if Joanne's husband were to tell her, "If you continue with your infidelity, you are no longer welcome in this house. You will have to move out. If you won't go, I will have no choice but to take the children and leave"? Such a stand would force Joanne to take a long, hard look at the value of her relationship with her family. Insisting on accountability is often the only thing that can save a marriage.

That is not to say that there is no place for forgiveness. Of course there is. Forgiveness is a cornerstone of Christ's message and a commandment to Christians. But the time for that is after the couple has reconciled, after a strong commitment to each other and to their marriage has been reaffirmed. Then there can be total forgiveness, a recognition of shared failures, and a mutual, prayerful reaffirmation before God of the vows that were taken and the promises that were made on their wedding day.

When confronted with marital unfaithfulness, a person may find it very difficult to think objectively. Reactions may well be influenced by the several myths that surround infidelity. It is crucial that we be able to separate the misconceptions from the facts that marriage counselors have learned in the course of their work. The following are some of the most accepted and destructive myths concerning infidelity, and the facts we now know about them:

Myth 1: A person has an affair because of the failure of his or her spouse.

Fact: Many husbands and wives blame themselves for their spouses' infidelities. The idea that a partner seeks extramarital affairs because of an unsatisfactory marriage relationship is probably the most common belief about infidelity.

Many unfaithful spouses do complain about their partners' failings. Yet, according to marriage counselors, the failings pointed out are usually exaggerated. Quite often they are not failings at all, but merely differences of opinion that haven't been talked out. At other times the dissatisfied partner simply had expectations that were unrealistically high.

Some people are unfaithful because of a need to prove their attractiveness to the opposite sex. This is especially true of middle-aged men, who often become involved in an affair in a panicked effort to recapture their lost youth.

Of course, unfaithful partners want their spouses to accept the blame for the adultery. So do the third parties involved, the so-called lovers. If the wronged spouses are willing to accept the blame, the unfaithful can continue with the affair and feel faultless in doing so.

The important thing to understand is that one partner cannot be responsible for the behavior of the other. People don't make each other do things. Husbands and wives who commit adultery do so because they have chosen to do so.

Myth 2: A person is better off not knowing about a spouse's affair.

Fact: If there is any degree of closeness in a marriage, the fact that there is something wrong cannot be hidden from a husband or wife. The inevitable decline in intimacy will in turn very likely encourage the infidelity; the more unhappy the marriage, the easier it is to rationalize the unfaithfulness.

It is always better for a suspicious partner to talk about any concerns—in a nonaccusative manner, of course. If the suspicion proves groundless, the honest discussion may help to uncover those other problems that actually are causing the concern. If the suspicion is true, the spouse is still better off. It's always easier to deal with facts than fantasy. With the truth out in the open, the couple can take steps to work out their problems. Furthermore, if it is out in the open it's less likely to happen again.

Myth 3: People who are unfaithful don't love their spouses.

Fact: This is not necessarily true. It is possible to love one person and still be infatuated with another. Many adulterous spouses are firmly committed to their marriages. That's why insisting that a spouse assume the responsibility for making and carrying out a commitment often works well toward reconciliation.

Myth 4: Affairs are fun.

Fact: Initially this is true. The excitement, the secrecy, the romantic feeling of "first love" all work together to give the sensational feeling that blinds people to their lovers' faults and takes them back to the days when they were young and first discovering love. But soon all this fades and reality sets in. Then the guilt and the pressure of deceit begin to overshadow the fun. With few exceptions, infidelity becomes an overpowering emotional burden for the unfaithful partner.

Myth 5: If a spouse gets caught cheating, the marriage has to end.

Fact: At first divorce may seem to be the only way out of a hopeless situation, but the truth is that divorce can initiate a whole new set of problems even more difficult to solve than the adultery itself. The majority of marriages are well worth saving.

There is an option: Forgiveness. Although it may seem impossible at first, most spouses discover that they are eventually able to find the strength to forgive the infidelity. There are those, however, who deliberately choose not to forgive. They say, "I can't," but what they mean is, "I won't." They cling to their hurt out of self-pity or because it makes them feel superior to their spouses or because it provides them with an effective weapon. One wife could induce her husband to agree to almost anything when she played her best shot: "You *should* go along with me on this after all you put me through. You owe me!"

Although forgiveness and reconciliation are the goals toward which intervention should aim, it is unrealistic to think that this will be achieved easily. In the end it is the unfaithful partner who determines how it will all end. If the guilty party's response is like that of Sue's husband, the chances of a reconciliation are much greater than if the erring partner assumes an attitude like Joanne's. The sin must be removed before the marriage can be healed, before loving affirmation and forgiveness can take place.

In some marriages, professional help may be needed to restore harmony. In others, with God's help, the couple can do it on their own. Either way, they should approach the problem with patience, honesty, and a desire to set things straight.

Infidelity is never good for a marriage. But neither does it have to be a deathblow. An affair can be the shock treatment that pushes a husband and wife into talking and listening to each other for the first time in years. There is seldom a truly romantic ending for families torn by infidelity. Many marriages are healed by God's power, and they do seem healthy. But sin always leaves scars.

Rebuilding trust in a marriage damaged by infidelity is perhaps the hardest task of all. A wise Christian couple will consider the forgiveness alternative before discarding the marriage. They will lay their difficulties before the Lord. Confession and forgiveness are foundations of Christian reconciliation. In the presence of the Lord the couple must examine their marriage, place it in a context of total commitment, and communicate openly.

This is a painful, humbling task. Yet, according to couples who have worked out their marriage difficulties and have successfully reconciled, the rewards of a renewed relationship are well worth the effort.

A QUICK OVERVIEW

Because infidelity is becoming increasingly accepted in our society, we can expect more and more people to come to us about this problem. Be prepared to be approached by women who have been unfaithful as well as by women who have been wronged.

Spouses involved in adultery are very adept at rationalizing, excusing their sin and, blaming their actions on others. Refuse to accept this. If you are talking to the unfaithful spouse, insist that she accept the responsibility for her actions. If you are talking to the wronged spouse, insist that she refuse to accept the blame. A strong emphasis should be placed on accountability.

Infidelity strikes a strong blow to the very foundation of a marriage that is supposedly based on mutual trust. But it does not have to be a deathblow. Rebuilding trust in a damaged marriage is a painful, humbling, and very difficult task, but it can be done. The key words are accountability, repentance, and forgiveness. (Consider chapter 11 for a deeper look into the subject of forgiveness and for Dos and Don'ts and Suggested Reading on that subject.)

Couples who have reconciled and have successfully worked out their marriage difficulties report that the rewards make the effort worthwhile.

DOS AND DON'TS

You will need to respond quite differently to an unfaithful wife than to the wife of an unfaithful man.

When a woman comes to you about her unfaithful spouse,

Do ...

- Encourage a suspicious partner to speak with her spouse about her concerns. This can be a starting point for a discussion of what actually happened, what it means, and what can be done to prevent it from happening again. If her suspicions are wrong, it can lead to discussion of other problems in the marriage.
- Suggest that the couple consult a qualified Christian marriage counselor. Remember, infidelity rarely causes marital problems; it occurs because problems are already there.
- Emphasize the importance of doing something *now*. The sooner the problem is faced, the greater the chance of saving the marriage.

- Help her to understand that she must come to terms with the hurt and anger she is feeling before she can make clear, rational decisions.
- Stress the importance of good communication in a marriage.
- Warn her not to scoff at her husband when he says he loves her. It may be true.
- Refuse to allow her to blame herself for her husband's behavior.
- Stress the importance of accountability on the part of the unfaithful spouse.
- Emphasize that while Scripture allows her freedom to divorce because of adultery, it will not necessarily be a solution to the problem. Divorce can spawn a whole new set of problems even more difficult to solve.
- Strongly suggest that she consider the alternative of forgiveness before discarding her marriage.
- Make it clear that the marriage is not necessarily over. Healing can take place.
- Emphasize the importance of forgiveness, "even as God for Christ's sake has forgiven you."
- Encourage her to be loving and forgiving after a reconciliation has taken place.

Don't ...

- Betray her trust by sharing her situation with others.
- Blame her for her husband's infidelity. Don't even suggest that she must have given him reason for his unfaithfulness.
- Suggest that she try to think of ways that she may have contributed to his infidelity.
- Encourage her to work toward changing her husband. She cannot do it.
- Encourage her to tolerate her husband's infidelity, to stand by him lovingly and patiently in hopes that he will shape up.
- Ask her to be patient in waiting for her husband to get over his infatuation with the "other woman."
- Try to diagnose the "underlying problem" that led to this situation. Leave this to a trained counselor.
- Encourage her to allow her unfaithful partner his rights as husband and father while he is still engaged in an adulterous affair. By his actions he has given up those rights as head of your home.

- Tell her she must be loving and nonjudgmental while the infidelity is still going on.

When a woman comes to you about her own infidelity,

Do ...

- Speak the truth in love, even if it hurts (Eph. 4:15,25)
- Insist that she take the responsibility for her own actions. She must not be allowed to shift the blame to someone else.
- Suggest that the couple seek marriage counseling from a qualified counselor.
- Emphasize the importance of her coming to the point where she can honestly ask for forgiveness from God and from her husband.
- Emphasize that she must not use sex as a battleground for problems in her marriage.
- Make it clear that a different sex partner will not make things better. Infidelity inevitably makes things worse.
- Make it clear that she cannot persist in an affair, or leave open the possibility of beginning another one, and still expect to continue in a satisfactory marriage relationship. She cannot have it both ways.
- Stress the importance of her seeking counseling from a qualified Christian counselor who will help her to determine why this problem has come about.
- Emphasize the importance of confession and a renewed commitment to faithfulness in her marriage.
- Make it clear that the marriage is not necessarily over. Healing can take place.
- Let her know that she has no right to expect her husband to be understanding and forgiving.
- Challenge her to avoid putting herself into a situation where she will be tempted. When temptation comes, she should immediately leave the situation and avoid getting into it again.
- Offer her your prayerful support.

Don't ...

- Hesitate to call her actions "sin." Whether she likes to hear it or not, that is exactly what it is.
- Ever be tolerant of deliberate and ongoing sin.

- Betray her trust by sharing her situation with others.
- Encourage her to expect her husband to stand by her lovingly and patiently in hopes that her feelings will change. Until she changes, she has no right to expect anything from her husband.
- Try to diagnose the underlying problem that led to the infidelity. Leave that for a trained counselor.
- Accept rationalization as to why God might be understanding about her relationship. God never puts His stamp of approval on sin.

SUGGESTED READING

Adams, Jay E. *Marriage, Divorce and Remarriage in the Bible*. Phillipsburg, N.J.: Presbyterian and Reformed, 1980.

Crabb, Lawrence J., Jr. *The Marriage Builder*. Grand Rapids: Zondervan, 1982.

Dobson, James C. *Love Must Be Tough*. Waco, Tex.: Word Books, 1983.

Stresses the idea of forcing an unfaithful partner to accept the responsibility for his actions.

Kuhne, Karen. *A Healing Season*. Grand Rapids: Zondervan, 1985.

The autobiography of an unfaithful Christian and her reconciliation with her husband.

Lutzer, Erwin W. *Living With Your Passions*. Wheaton, Ill.: Victor Books, 1983.

A how-to book useful for individual reading or for group study. A leader's guide available.

Murray, John. *Divorce*. Philadelphia: Presbyterian and Reformed, 1961.

Peterson, J. Allan. *The Myth of the Greener Grass*. Wheaton, Ill.: Tyndale House, 1983.

A scriptural guide to the dilemma of infidelity within the Christian community. Includes a unique self-test designed separately for husbands and wives.

Wheat, Ed. *How to Save Your Marriage Alone*. Grand Rapids: Zondervan, 1983.

LOCAL REFERENCES

MARRIAGE COUNSELORS

Christian counselors are preferable. If none are available, be certain that the philosophy of the counselor chosen is compatible with Christian and biblical principles.

NAME:

Number:

Notes:

NAME:

Number:

Notes:

MINISTER TRAINED IN MARITAL COUNSELING

Not all ministers have the special training needed to handle marriage counseling. If there is one in your area who does, he would be a good addition to your local resource list.

NAME:

Number:

Notes:

7.

Rape

You are walking toward your office door when a hysterical woman runs up to meet you. "You've got to help me!" she cries. "I don't know what to do! Please help me!"

Quickly you usher her into your office. Although it is a warm morning, she is wearing a large coat that she pulls tightly around her. Her hair is disheveled and her makeup smeared. Shock and terror show on her face.

You help the woman into a chair and get her a glass of water. She struggles to gain her composure. When she has calmed down a bit, you encourage her to tell you what happened.

"It was terrible!" she says. "I never even saw him coming. He just grabbed me!" She starts to cry again. "I feel so dirty, so guilty!"

Suddenly, with shocking clarity, you understand what has happened. This woman has been raped. You want to comfort her, to ease her pain, but you can't think of a single appropriate thing to say.

Many Christians find it difficult even to say the word "rape," yet it is dreaded by women more deeply than anything else, a "fate worse than death." That fear seems to be well-founded. Using conservative estimates, experts calculate that a woman's chance of being raped at some point during her life is an appalling one in ten. Statistics reveal that in our country a woman is raped every eight minutes.

You ask the woman if she was sexually assaulted. She nods her head.

"It happened this morning," she tells you through her tears. "I work the early shift at the restaurant. Since it's only three blocks away, I usually walk. This morning I left around five-thirty as usual. I wasn't quite a block away when a man suddenly jumped out of the bushes and grabbed me. He put his hand over my mouth and held a knife to my throat. I couldn't think straight. I was certain that he was going to kill me.

"I wanted to scream, to kick, to fight, but the man said he'd kill me if I resisted. I had no doubt that he meant everything he said." Shuddering with the terrible memory, she adds, "Maybe it would have been better if he *had* killed me. I'll never be the same again."

Surrounded by Myths

Unlike robbery or mugging, sexual assault takes something irreplaceable from a woman. The victim and usually her family also are plunged into a crisis that surpasses anything they have ever known. The trauma caused by this violent crime will not pass quickly or easily. Studies indicate that it takes from six months to six years for rape victims to feel normal again—if they ever do. Christian rape victims are no exception. Their suffering is as great as anyone else's, their faith notwithstanding.

The distraught woman insists that her life has been changed forever, that she will never again be the same. Undoubtedly the days following the sexual attack will be difficult for her. They are for all rape victims. Like the woman in your office, victims of sexual assault often complain of feeling "dirty," guilty, and ashamed.

Frequently they are haunted by nightmares and plagued with depression. They become obsessively concerned for their safety. Trust and intimacy come hard. Even worse are their feelings of hopelessness about their future. Breakups of relationships are common. So are suicide attempts. For Christians, many times there is also a crisis of faith. "Why would God let this happen to me?" is a question that we as counselors will confront. (For suggestions on handling this, see chapter 11.)

You look at the plain, somewhat plump, almost middle-aged woman sitting slumped in the chair before you. You realize there is no such thing as a typical victim. Some are young: children. Some are old: great-grandmothers. Some are beautiful and some are plain. Women of all ages, classes, races, religions, and educational levels fall prey to rapists.

As with many other crisis situations, myths abound where rape is concerned:

— Only attractive, provocative women, usually ones who have already earned themselves bad reputations, get raped.
— Nice girls who stay home at night and refuse to talk to strangers don't.
— Secretly every woman wants to get raped.
— Men rape because they are sex-starved and can't control their passion.
— Most rapists are sick perverts.
— Rapists are usually put behind bars.

Not one of these statements is true. Who gets raped? Old women and little children, educated and illiterate, rich and poor, comely or homely. No woman is immune to the threat.

Humiliated, damaged in body and spirit, it takes rape victims a long, long time to recover completely. Some never do.

What drives a man to rape a woman? Experts tell us that, rather than being a crime motivated by sexual desire, rape is one in which sex is used as a weapon to harm and humiliate the victim. Sometimes rape is a way of expressing anger that is directed toward the entire female sex. When this is the case, the attack often includes a beating. Are the men who commit such crimes crazy or psychotic? Sometimes. Rapists, like victims, don't fit stereotypes. In more than a third of the reported cases they are friends, relatives, or neighbors, who assault their victims in the garage, the laundry room, or their own homes. In other cases the attackers are strangers who select their victims at random. Are most rapists convicted and jailed? Hardly. Most are not even reported.

The image of a man who is consumed by an uncontrollable, and sometimes understandable, lust being enticed by a provocative woman wearing sexy clothes is fading. So is the belief that women falsely cry rape to cover up their own misdeeds.

But myths die hard. Many people still place the bulk of the blame for a sexual attack on the woman. Through the centuries, laws have implied that rape victims are somehow guilty. Women were expected to produce physical injuries proving that they fought back—the psychological trauma they suffered was not injury enough. Defense lawyers were fond of using Balzac's celebrated statement on rape: "One cannot thread a needle when the needle doesn't stand still."

"I knew I should fight him," the woman says again. "And I wanted to, I really did. But I was so afraid." Then she adds bitterly, "Now everyone will blame me for what happened. Since I didn't get myself killed fighting back, I wanted it, right?"

Wrong. You assure her you have no doubt but that she did all she could.

Even if he isn't armed, there is no way of knowing how a given attacker will respond. One rapist in therapy said that as soon as a woman cried, he would immediately let her go. But another man in the same group said that if a woman became assertive, he would stab her.

That's not to say that it is always wrong for a woman to try to protect herself. It is usually recommended that she first try talking and reasoning with her attacker, but fighting may be the best action if talking fails. Yet the woman must keep in mind that if her attempt is unsuccessful, it can stimulate her attacker to even greater violence. Should she choose to resist actively, she must give it an all-out effort.

There are some situations—as when the attacker is holding a knife or gun—in which a woman should never attempt to fight back.

In the end it is the shocked and terrified woman herself who must decide how to react to a sexual attack, and her decision must be made in the first few seconds. That decision should depend on the circumstances: Is her attacker armed? Is he beyond reasoning? Will she most likely be killed if she does not submit? In a moment of extreme stress she must determine what the attacker wants from her and to what lengths he will go to get it.

The woman in your office possibly is alive simply because she *didn't* fight back.

Changed Laws, Changing Attitudes

Since the early 1970s almost every state has made major changes in its rape laws. The legal view of rape has changed from a violent expression of sex to a sexual expression of violence. The ramifications for victims are great.

This change of emphasis is also helping us to understand the seeming inconsistency in the life of many rapists. Case in point: A thirty-two-year-old man, later convicted of rape, worked by day as a desk clerk in a retirement hotel and a volunteer leader of a young adults group in his church. But by night he was a different person, a rapist who prowled the streets of a neat, middle-class neighborhood on the edge of Hollywood. According to police, he raped as many as one hundred women ranging in age from twenty-four to seventy-one.

You ask the woman to continue with her story.

"When the man finally left, I crawled back home," she says. "All I wanted to do was lock the doors, take a hot bath and scrub myself all over with strong soap, and curl up in bed with the blankets pulled over my head. But then I started thinking about that horrible man, that he was probably going to attack somebody else. Suddenly, more than anything else, I wanted him caught."

Many women refuse to report rape. According to surveys taken by the U.S. Census Bureau, the FBI, and the National Opinion Research Center, only 3 to 10 percent of all rapes are reported. Some women refuse to report an attack out of shame for what has happened. Others are afraid of being stigmatized or accused of provoking the attack. Because so few victims prosecute, rapists are emboldened and feel they are free to do as they want. Many experts are convinced that if more men were prosecuted, fewer rapes would occur.

The crime that women are most reluctant to report is "acquaintance rape" or "date rape." When the victim has had social dealings with her attacker, it is much more likely that she will be blamed for provoking the rape.

But times are changing. Increasingly, rape victims are refusing to withdraw and suffer in silent horror and shame. Nor are they willing to accept any part of the blame for what happened to them. Legal reforms are helping, along with pressure for more convictions and stiffer sentences for rapists.

Not long ago, women complained that the subsequent medical examination was almost as bad as the rape itself and that the responding police officer was rough, insensitive, and accusing. Fortunately there is a definite trend toward a more enlightened and sympathetic approach by doctors and police officers. Often the behavior of the first person a victim sees after her attack can either ease or add to the shock and humiliation. The chances of emotional recovery are far greater when the victim at that moment receives the help and support she so desperately needs.

This new openness is having another result: more and more Christian workers—men and women like you—are being called upon to meet crisis situations involving rape victims. These counselors must understand the importance of their response and attitude toward these women.

"I don't know what to think, what to feel," the woman tells you. "I guess I'm in shock. I hate the man who did this to me, and yet I know that it is a sin to hate. I want him caught and punished, and yet I know that I should leave vengeance to the Lord. And as for the feelings I have toward God right now . . . well, I'm not at all sure about them either. God could have kept me safe from this if He had wanted to."

You tell the woman that she has every right to feel angry. You acknowledge the fact that it will take her a while to sort out her feelings. She has a lot to work through. Often neighbors and friends, or even her own family, won't understand. Overcoming her humiliation, her sense of guilt, her feeling of being dirty—this is not easy to accomplish.

Almost without exception, victims of rape need professional counseling. This extra help will hasten the healing process. Those who are not allowed to express their feelings of anger and frustration tend to turn them inward. Many suffer for years after a sexual assault.

"I'll never be the same," the tearful woman tells you in despair. "If I live to be one hundred, I'll never recover from the horror of this day."

You agree that it is unlikely that she will ever forget what happened. No one expects her to. But the time will come, you assure her, when the horror of this day will no longer dominate her life, when she will not think about it every day. It will take a while, perhaps a long time, and it will take a lot of work, but healing can come.

You tell her that although you cannot explain why God allowed this to happen, you know that He does care about her. And although this experience has been shattering beyond understanding, through God's power her recovery can be complete.

You have one more thing to tell the woman: the attack *must* be reported. You offer to call the police or, if she would prefer, someone who can accompany her through the ordeal of reporting the crime, answering the necessary questions, and getting a medical examination.

"Could you call my sister?" she asks. "I would like to have her with me."

You make the call. While you wait for her sister's arrival you pray together, thanking God for sparing this woman's life and asking for His strength and comfort and healing for her.

By the time her sister arrives, the woman's tears are dried. "Maybe I will make it after all," she says.

A QUICK OVERVIEW

The very word "rape" strikes terror into the hearts of most women, with good reason. Experts say that one in ten women will fall prey to a rapist at some time during her life. No woman—young or old, rich or poor, educated or illiterate, good or bad—is immune.

Public pressure has resulted in more rape convictions and increased respect for victims in the last decade. Police officers and doctors, often the first people to see victims of attack, are taking a more enlightened and sympathetic approach in their dealings with them.

But damaging misconceptions about women and rape persist. Perhaps the worst of these is the idea that the victim is in some way responsible for provoking the attack.

Most sexual attacks are never reported. This not only can deprive a victim of the help she needs, but also leaves the attacker free to commit the crime again.

Understandably, rape victims suffer feelings of despair, anger, frustration, and helplessness. It is important that they receive professional counseling to help them toward healing.

DOS AND DON'TS

Because of the stereotypes associated with rape, rapists, and their victims, and the stigma generally attached to the crime, we need to be very careful in our dealings with a victim. It is our responsibility to set her on the road to healing.

Do ...

- React with sensitivity.
- Avoid evaluating the victim according to a preconceived stereotype of what kind of women get raped.
- Avoid pressing for details of the sexual attack.
- Try substituting the term "sexual assault" if the word "rape" is uncomfortable. This less offensive term may make it easier for the victim to talk about it.
- Let her know that in some circumstances it is definitely better to give in to the attacker than to resist.
- Affirm that, under the circumstances, the victim did everything she could to resist the attack.
- Assure her that the rape was not her fault. She has no reason to feel guilty.
- Encourage her to write down the details of what happened. She may find it easier to remember and express specifics if she is not under the pressure and embarrassment of talking about the attack.
- Suggest that she write out her feelings. Writing can be highly therapeutic, and she may well find that she can put down on paper words that she cannot bring herself to speak.
- Everything you can to persuade the victim to report the crime.
- Encourage her to go to the police or a hospital emergency room immediately if the rape has just occurred. Only then will

the police be able to get the physical evidence needed to convict her attacker.

- Encourage her to gather evidence even if she is certain that she doesn't want to press charges. She may change her mind.
- Arrange for a sympathetic, supportive person to accompany her through the ordeal of reporting the attack to the police and going to the hospital emergency room.
- Arrange for someone to care for her children while she is gone.
- Encourage her to see a professional counselor. She needs to talk to someone who can help her work through her feelings and fears.
- Affirm God's power to heal and restore, however shattering her experience.

Don't ...

- React with visible shock, horror, or disgust.
- Accuse her of being even partially to blame. Even if you think this may be true, your job is to be supportive, not judgmental.
- Offer superficial or simplistic answers.
- Discourage her from reporting the rape, regardless of the circumstances. The crimes hardest to report are those committed by family members, friends, or acquaintances. But for her own recovery, and for the protection of future victims, it is vital that she report the crime.
- Criticize her for not resisting hard enough.
- Even hint that she might have been spared had she asked God for help. The ways of God are not so simple or clear-cut, and she doesn't need the burden of additional feelings of guilt.
- Urge the victim to forgive her attacker. Forgiving takes time.

RESOURCES

National Coalition Against Sexual Assault (NCASA)

Northwest: Albany County Rape Crisis Center
          112 State Street, Room 640
          Albany, NY 12207

Southeast: 5495 Murray
         Memphis, TN 38119

Midwest: Loop YWCA/Women's Services
37 South Wabash
Chicago, IL 60603

South: National Office
Austin Rape Crisis Center
P.O. Box 7156
Austin, TX 78713

West: 416 South 25 Street
Laramie, WY 82070

Far West: Office of Criminal Justice Planning
9719 Lincoln Village Drive
Sacramento, CA 95827

Women Against Rape. For free information about projects in your area, send a self-addressed, stamped envelope to this organization at:

P.O. Box 02084
Columbus, OH 43202

Self-Defense

Specific information on easy-to-learn self-defense tactics for women are available from the following address. Besides the book *The Rational Woman's Guide to Self-Defense*, there is a film, *Common Sense Self-Defense*.

Department of Physical Education
California State University at Los Angeles
5151 State University Drive
Los Angeles, CA 90032

SUGGESTED READING

Fortune, Marie M. *Sexual Violence: The Unmentionable Sin*. New York: Pilgrim, 1983.

Written by a Protestant minister who has worked for several years with the Center for the Prevention of Sexual and Domestic Violence. Includes a section on practical strategies for Christian ministers in dealing with victims of rape, domestic violence, and child molestation. Also covers working with the offenders.

How to Protect Yourself Against Sexual Assault. Justice Department, Consumer Information Center, Dept. 44, Pueblo, CO 81009.

Contains much information, including agencies and services for rape victims.

Roberts, Deborah. *Raped*. Grand Rapids: Zondervan, 1981.

The autobiography of a Christian rape victim.

The Rational Woman's Guide to Self-Defense. Department of Physical Education, California State University at Los Angeles, 5151 State University Drive, Los Angeles, CA 90032.

LOCAL REFERENCES

POLICE DEPARTMENT

Many police departments have an officer who specializes in sexual assault crimes. If this is so in your area, be sure you have the name of that person.

NAME:

Number:

Notes:

HOSPITAL EMERGENCY ROOM

You can call ahead and alert the emergency room staff that a rape victim is on the way. This may save her embarrassment and delays when she arrives.

HOSPITAL:

Number:

HOSPITAL:

Number:

108

HOSPITAL:

Number:

LOCAL RAPE CRISIS CENTER

There are almost one thousand of these centers nationwide.

NUMBER:

Contact Person:

Notes:

HOTLINE

Most rape crisis centers operate a hotline with counselors on call twenty-four hours a day. Even if there is not a Rape Crisis Center in your community, you can locate the hotline associated with the one closest to you. The counselors will be very helpful in guiding you.

NUMBER:

Notes:

NUMBER:

Notes:

SUPPORT GROUPS

These are forming throughout the country.

NUMBER:

Contact Person:

Notes:

NUMBER:

Contact Person:

Notes:

COUNSELORS

Choose one or more who are experienced in working with rape victims.

NAME:

Number:

Notes:

NAME:

Number:

Notes:

SUPPORT PEOPLE

Christian women can help by being available to accompany the victim through the reporting process and the subsequent medical examination. Check ahead of time with some who you think would be especially helpful and ask if they would be willing to be included on your list. Try to compile several names.

NAME:

Number:

Notes:

NAME:

Number:

Notes:

NAME:

Number:

Notes:

8. *Suicide*

The two young women come in together. You know Laura Evans, but not the person with her.

"This is my friend Melody," Laura says. "She didn't want to come today, but I told her she really should talk to someone."

You shake Melody's hand and tell her you are glad she came. You pull up chairs for the two women and wait for someone to tell you what concern has brought them to see you.

Melody sits in silence, staring down at her hands. Laura looks over at her friend, then at you.

"Melody says she tried to kill herself," Laura tells you. "She called me and said she had swallowed a bunch of pills. I called an ambulance, then rushed over to her apartment. But when I got there she seemed fine. She was sitting on her bed talking to the paramedics. They didn't even take her to the hospital."

Melody suddenly sits erect, her eyes flashing. "I *did* try to kill myself!" she insists. "But I failed, just like in everything else I try. I swallowed every pill in the medicine cabinet, but all there was were aspirin and over-the-counter medicines. I guess they weren't potent enough to do the job."

Whether or not Melody made a legitimate suicide attempt is impossible for you to determine, but one thing is certain—she wants both you and Laura to take the matter seriously. You ask Melody to tell you about herself.

"What's there to tell?" she says in a weary voice. "Every morning I drag myself out of bed and go to work. After putting in a day that seems twenty hours long, I come home and heat up a bowl of soup for dinner. Some nights I go right to bed and sleep for twelve or thirteen hours. Other nights I can't sleep at all, so I lay on the couch listening to music all night. Either way I'm so exhausted in the morning that it takes every bit of strength I can muster just to get myself out of bed.

"That's my life," she concludes with a sigh. "Every day is the same, only a little bit worse. I can't go on like this. You tell me, what have I got to live for?"

You ask her about her friends, her hobbies, the activities she enjoys.

"I don't have any friends," she answers flatly. "None except Laura, that is, and she only puts up with me because she's too nice to tell me to get lost. We both know that she'd be better off without me around."

Laura starts to protest, but Melody doesn't give her the chance. "I used to like to jog, and I did some painting, but I don't do either one anymore. It just seems like too much of an effort to get started on anything."

Living Under a Cloud

In America suicide has reached epidemic proportions; it is now the eighth leading cause of death. For women, the ages between forty and fifty-nine produce the most suicides. But adults are by no means the only ones who do away with themselves. The suicide rate among adolescents has tripled in the last generation. In 1980, one in every five suicides involved young people between the ages of fifteen and twenty-four. For this age group, it is the second leading cause of death. Nor are children immune. Between the ages of eight and fourteen, suicide is the eighth leading cause of death. And as if these statistics are not shocking enough, psychiatrists estimate that for every documented suicide there are many more undetected that go down as accidental deaths, especially fatal auto crashes.

Men, women, teenagers, senior citizens, children—they are dying at their own hands at an alarming rate. Why do they do it? They do it because their lives become unbearable. Suicide expresses not so much a desire to die as a desperate attempt to get away from the pain of living.

You ask Melody why she decided to end her life.

"Why not?" she responds with a weary sigh. "I'm lonesome and I'm tired, and no one cares anyway."

"Don't you think it's really because of your depression, Melody?" Laura asks. "You know how you get when you're down. You don't see things the way they really are. I happen to know that a lot of people care much more than you give them credit for."

Laura's assessment is probably right on target. Of all the people who take their own lives, an estimated 60 percent are judged to be clinically depressed. For most people in depression, the cloud lifts and they get on with their lives. But for those deeply ensnared in its web, depression can be a debilitating disorder. It infects both the body and the mind with a lingering, soul-destroying sadness that causes feelings of worthlessness and despondency such as Melody has expressed.

Many of the other symptoms Melody described also fit in with Laura's diagnosis of depression: her sleep problems, headaches, fatigue. People suffering from depression no longer care about normal daily activities. They can't understand what is happening; they only know that something has gone terribly wrong.

Because Melody seems embarrassed about the reference to depression, you feel certain that she would never have mentioned it herself. Perhaps she, like many others, considers it a sign of mental weakness. It is this misconception that causes so many depressed people to remain untreated.

You tell Melody that depression is no cause for embarrassment, that in many cases it is not psychological at all. It may be a physical problem, one that can be treated successfully.

The Causes of Suicide

Actually suicide is seldom the result of any single cause. There are many contributing factors. In adolescents, for instance, feelings of turmoil and alienation are greatly intensified by today's shifting values. Now, more than ever before, people of all ages need stability and support from their families, friends, and communities. Yet they are finding it less.

Society tells us to press for a quick solution for every problem and an end to every discomfort. Perhaps that's why more and more people are convinced that if they have a problem that is not easily solved, the only way out is death. Young people aren't learning coping skills, nor do they recognize that circumstances will change. They don't understand that pain and loneliness will not be with them forever, that things really can and do get better.

Because most suicidal people are unable to communicate well enough to let other people know how they really feel, family and friends are often unaware of the suffering and despair they are feeling. Many of their acquaintances think that their lives are going along just fine. Other people have no way of knowing what is going on inside the heads of those who are suffering.

"I didn't even get a promotion this year," Melody tells you. "Another woman who has only been in the office six months got moved up instead of me."

Laura tells you that the suicide attempt occurred only two days after Melody was passed over for promotion. Evidently this was the triggering incident. A triggering incident is not always so obvious, however. In fact, it may be a deceptively minor event—an argument, perhaps, or a best friend's moving away, or a poor grade in school. Though they seem minor to you, to the susceptible person these can be perceived as insurmountable failures or embarrassments.

Personal struggles can appear even more futile when the outside world seems no better off. Every day we are bombarded with news of terrorism in the Middle East, starvation in Africa, murder and muggings in our own country, and natural disasters around the world. Through television, violence has become an accepted condition of life in America. By the time she enters college, the average child will have seen 17,000 violent deaths on TV. Even more ominous is the ever-present fear of a nuclear holocaust. It's hard to reach out for a future in a world that seems to hold no future.

Still, it is difficult to understand why so many people take their own lives. The rest of us live under these same pressures, yet most of us don't try to kill ourselves. Although it is hard for those who are not suicidal to understand, suicide is the end result of a complex interaction of personal, social, and psychological factors that progressively tighten around a person into a choking knot from which she can find no escape.

From the first it was obvious that Laura was not at all convinced that Melody really did intend to kill herself. And Laura's doubts may be well-founded. Experts agree that many people who attempt suicide really want to live. If they could find another way to solve their problems, they would. What they really want to do is change their lives in order to make them worth living. The problem is that these people suffer from a kind of "tunnel vision." It's as if they are looking down a long, dark tunnel where they can see nothing but darkness. Not knowing where they are in the tunnel, they think it must surely go on forever. They don't realize that there is light outside and that there is an end to the tunnel.

Because depression is often caused by a physical condition, you suggest that Melody see a medical doctor. You tell her that you will call and make an appointment for her if she agrees to go see him. Laura volunteers to drive her there.

"I'll go," Melody agrees with a sigh.

You call a physician with whom you are acquainted. When you have explained Melody's situation, he agrees to see her immediately.

After a word of prayer together, Melody and Laura leave, Laura's arm firmly around her friend's shoulders.

Reason for Hope

You can't get Melody out of your mind. You're still thinking about her when Laura stops by several hours later.

"They're going to put Melody in the hospital for a couple of days," Laura tells you. "For observation, they say. I sure hope she will be all right."

You tell Laura that you are glad to have a chance to talk with her alone. You thank her for being so concerned about her friend, for being willing to bring her to talk to you and to take her to the hospital.

"Melody really does think no one cares about her," Laura tells you. "I know that a lot of bad things are happening in her life right now—the promotion thing at work, a breakup with her boyfriend, family problems. . . ."

With such unsettling circumstances in her life, Melody's suicide attempt may be easier to understand than those of some others who seem to have everything going for them. The inescapable fact is that money, security, personal attractiveness—the things our society considers of greatest value—are failing us. The characteristics of self-esteem, love, faith, peace, fulfillment, and joy are far more important and enduring, but they are also more difficult to come by. The lack of fulfillment from these latter values leads to despair, an utter lack of hope. And it is despair that is the root cause of suicide.

"Do you think Melody really intended to kill herself?" Laura asks you.

You tell her that you have no way of knowing for certain. It may well have been merely a gesture engineered in such a way that she was sure to be rescued. But whether or not she intended to die, Melody was surely crying out for help. Her actions must be taken seriously. One of the most dangerous myths about suicide is that people who make threats or "attempts" that are not really intended to end in death never actually will kill themselves. These people certainly must be taken seriously, because they are *very* serious. Their threats and attempts may well be last-resort pleas for help.

"What if she tries something after she comes home?" Laura asks. "I feel responsible for her."

You tell Laura that it's important that she do her best to be there for Melody when she needs support, but that it is unrealistic to think that she can watch her friend twenty-four hours a day. If Melody is determined to kill herself, no one can stop her. Laura's responsibility is to support and encourage, and to do all she can to persuade Melody to enter therapy with a trained psychiatrist or psychologist.

Laura sits silently for a few minutes. "Poor Melody!" she says finally. "What will become of her? Do you think there is any hope?"

The answer, of course, is yes. No matter what the problem, no matter how great the hurt, there is always hope. The fact that Melody reached out to Laura is itself reason for hope. Her willingness to come to you, and to go to the hospital for help, are further signs that she wants and will accept help. People who truly want to die don't do those kinds of constructive things; they just die.

Danger Signals

Few suicides happen "out of the blue." Although they often go unrecognized, there are almost always danger signs. Experts agree that if more people were able to discern the warning signs, more help could be offered suicidal people.

The following is a list of danger signals for which friends and family members should be on the alert:

- Preoccupation with death, dying, or suicide
- Severe depression
- Withdrawal from friends and family
- Major changes in behavior
- Complaints about physical symptoms that can often be related to emotions—stomachache, headache, fatigue
- Sudden and extreme changes in eating habits, losing or gaining weight
- Constant feelings of worthlessness or self-hatred
- Persistent boredom
- Difficulty in concentrating, agitation, or inability to sit still
- Lack of interest in the future
- Unusual neglect of personal appearance
- Changes in sleeping patterns—too much or too little
- Radical personality changes such as excessive risk-taking
- Sudden outbursts of fury
- Unexplained loss of energy, lethargy, or excessive fatigue
- Withdrawal into apathy and helplessness

- Drug and/or alcohol use*
- Lost interest in the hobbies and activities that were once considered important
- Making "final arrangements" such as giving away prized possessions
- Cries for help, such as suicide threats or attempts

A person who is planning to commit suicide may also:

- Give verbal hints. These are statements such as "I won't be bothering you much longer" or "Nothing matters anymore" or "The world would be better off without me."
- Ask questions about suicide. An adolescent, for example, might ask a parent if he or she ever considered it. A good response to such a question would be, "Are you thinking about it? What thoughts do you have?" This will open the subject for discussion.
- Put her affairs in order. For example, the person might give away prized possessions, write a will, or throw belongings away.
- Become suddenly cheerful after a period of depression. This could indicate that she has made a decision to end it all.

These characteristics are only generalizations, of course. Don't think that a person who doesn't fit them is automatically out of danger. It is far better to err on the side of overreacting than to ignore a danger signal.

A QUICK OVERVIEW

Women, men, teenagers, senior citizens, and even children are dying by their own hands at an alarming rate. People commit suicide because their lives have become unbearable. It is not so much that they truly want to die as it is a desperate attempt to escape the pain of living.

Many people who consider suicide simply don't have anyone to whom they can turn. A lot of bad things are happening in their lives. They have no resources to help them handle their problems, and they become extremely depressed. What they need most is some sense of hope, a promise that something better lies ahead.

---

*While drugs and alcohol don't cause suicide, alcohol and certain kinds of drugs are depressants. Using them will increase the severity of a depression.

If a person's pain can be found and treated, the suicide can often be prevented. Effective counseling of a suicidal person depends on the counselor's ability to determine the motivation behind the act. The roots of depression lie deep and cannot be dug up either quickly or easily. Unless we are counselors specifically trained in suicide intervention, we should not tackle such a difficult, time-consuming, and critical counseling assignment. As crisis counselors, we should have as our goal getting the desperate person the professional help she needs.

Suicide is a terrible waste. Crisis is temporary, but death is final. Take every threat of suicide seriously. Offer what comfort and hope you can. But most of all, get help.

DOS AND DON'TS

When we are dealing with a suicidal person, our goal should be to bring her together with an agency or counselor who can give her the in-depth, supportive help she desperately needs. Because she may feel that no one cares about her, our attitudes of loving acceptance and true concern can literally make the difference between life and death.

Do ...

- Get the person to a medical facility immediately if there is any indication that she has taken medicine or poison.
- Ask questions and show a willingness to listen.
- Allow the depressed person to talk openly, without criticism or judgment, about her anguished feelings. Questions like "What is causing your feelings?" and "How long have you felt this way?" are nonjudgmental but will allow her to vent her feelings.
- Be patient and supportive.
- Make a distinction between ordinary moodiness and clinical depression.
- Understand that even children can get depressed enough to kill themselves.
- Emphasize that depression is not a sign of mental weakness or sin.
- Assure the hurting person that it is in no way unspiritual, nor does it indicate a sign of lack of faith, to seek the help of a professional in dealing with depression. Let her know that she is by no means alone, that many others share her problem.

120

- Assure her that if she can just hang on, the unbearable pain will pass. Remind her that suicide is a permanent, irreversible solution to a temporary problem.
- Remind her that, no matter how great the hurt, there is always hope. There are many steps she can take to make her life better.
- Acknowledge the fact that the world can be a terrifying place, but that doesn't mean we need to give up in despair. Through God we have hope for the future and a promise concerning His sovereign control of it.
- Assure her that God will never leave her nor forsake her, that He will help her through this most difficult time in her life.
- Point out that, whatever her circumstances or problems, other options are open to her. Help her to discover acceptable, constructive ways to respond to her problems.
- Remind her of the many people who would suffer if she should carry out her suicide plan.
- Make sure the woman seeks professional help.
- Insist that a family member or friend of an uncooperative suicidal person persevere in getting the depressed person to a clinic or treatment center for help.
- Advise the family to be certain that the suicidal person has no ready access to guns, medicines, or poison.
- Explore with the family sources of stress, tension, and anger. Strongly suggest that the whole family receive counseling.
- Extend your support, and if possible that of the church, to the affected family.
- Follow up on the progress of the suicidal person. She needs to know that you really care.
- Uphold her and her family in prayer.

Don't . . .

- Minimize a suicidal threat or attempt. It is not up to you to decide whether or not the person will really kill herself. A threat should *always* be taken seriously.
- Allow the affected person to "swear you to secrecy." A person who comes to you, or who allows someone to bring her, is asking for help in the only way she can.
- Fault the parents for the depression of a child or teenager.
- Attempt to change the outlook of a depressed person by

admonishing her to "cheer up" or to "think about all those who are worse off than you." She would love to "cheer up" if only she could.

- Say that Christians have no right to be depressed. Such condemning remarks don't help at all.
- Attempt to counsel a suicidal person. She needs professional help that is usually long-term and time-consuming and requires specific training.
- Minimize the depth of the suffering she is experiencing.
- Assure her that her problems will be quickly, easily, or permanently overcome. They may be, but they may not. If not, her disappointment and increased guilt can devastate her even further.
- Be the one to initiate the involuntary commitment of an uncooperative suicidal person. If the person is not willing to seek help, then her nearest relative or the police should be advised to take care of the situation.

RESOURCES

Resource material about depression and suicide is available from:

National Institute of Mental Health

5600 Fisher Lane
Parklawn Bldg., Room 15C17
Rockville, MD 20857
(301) 443–4513

National Mental Health Association

1800 North Kent Street
Arlington, VA 22209
(703) 528–6405

SUGGESTED READING

Baker, Don, and Emery Nester. *Finding Hope and Meaning in Life's Darkest Shadow.* Portland, Ore.: Multnomah Press, Critical Concern Series, 1983.
Blackburn, Bill. *What You Should Know About Suicide.* Waco, Tex.: Word Books.
Davis, Creath. *Lord, If I Ever Needed You, It's Now.* Palm Springs, Calif.: Ronald N. Haynes.

A look at coping with grief, depression, doubts, despair, and deep agony that includes hope, promise, and scriptural insights.

Horton, Marilee. *Dear Mamma, Please Don't Die*. Nashville: Thomas Nelson, 1982.

The true story of a harrowing suicide attempt that leads to Christian insights on how to combat depression and rely on God.

Klagsbrun, Francine. *Too Young to Die: Youth and Suicide*. Boston: Houghton Mifflin, 1984.

LaHaye, Tim, *How to Win Over Depression*. Grand Rapids: Zondervan, 1976.

Maughon, Martha. *Why Am I Crying?* Grand Rapids: Zondervan, 1983.

Minirth, Frank B., and Paul D. Meier. *Happiness Is a Choice: A Manual on the Symptoms, Causes and Cures of Depression*. Grand Rapids: Baker, 1978.

Page, Carole Gift. *Neeley Never Said Goodbye*. Chicago: Moody Press, Sensitive Issues Series, 1984.

A fourteen-year-old learns to deal with her grief after her older brother's suicide. In confusion and anger she considers suicide for herself, but finds that God is strong enough to bring her through the tragedy of her brother's death. For adolescents.

White, John. *A Christian Physician Looks at Depression and Suicide*. Downers Grove, Ill.: InterVarsity, 1982.

Wright, Norman. *Now I Know Why I'm Depressed*. Eugene, Ore.: Harvest House, 1985.

An encouraging look at depression from a biblical perspective.

Yancey, Philip. *Where Is God When It Hurts?* Grand Rapids: Zondervan, 1977.

LOCAL REFERENCES

LOCAL CRISIS-INTERVENTION HOTLINE

Number:

Notes:

SUICIDE PREVENTION CENTER

These are present in most communities. Check the telephone directory or consult the police department.

NAME:

Number:

Contact Person:

MEDICAL DOCTORS, PSYCHOLOGISTS, PSYCHIATRISTS

It is best if you can locate Christian professionals. If this is not possible, choose ones who will uphold and affirm Christian principles.

NAME:

Specialty:

Number:

Notes:

NAME:

Specialty:

Number:

Notes:

NAME:

Specialty:

Number:

Notes:

9. Teenage Pregnancy

Impatient and obviously upset, Mrs. Simpson abruptly ushers her sixteen-year-old daughter Stephanie into your office. Stephanie slumps into the chair you indicate. Her mother sits stiffly next to her.

"Go ahead, Stephanie," Mrs. Simpson says in a strained voice. "It's your problem. You tell about it."

Stephanie sinks even lower into her chair and says nothing.

"She's probably too embarrassed to tell you," Mrs. Simpson says bitterly. "She should be. Stephanie is pregnant."

Teenage pregnancy, unwanted and unplanned, is a tragedy for everyone involved. It is quickly becoming a national tragedy as well. The statistics are plentiful and uncomfortable, even shocking. It is estimated that four out of ten girls who are now fourteen years old will become pregnant before they reach the age of twenty. One million young women between the ages of twelve and nineteen become pregnant every year in the United States, some thirty thousand of them fourteen and younger. A large majority of these girls are unmarried. American *children* are having children at a rate of 1,540 per day, about sixty-four every hour.

Because the number of sexually active teenagers (already about 41 percent, research suggests) continues to increase, and because an increase in teenage pregnancy is an inevitable result of this sexual activity, we can expect to encounter situations like Stephanie's.

The ramifications of teenage pregnancy are tragic indeed, often permanently altering the course of a young person's life. It is the main cause of eight out of ten high school dropouts. Teenage mothers are more likely to suffer from pregnancy-related health problems, and the infant mortality rate among babies born to them is nearly twice that of babies born to women in their twenties.

Sex outside marriage is a sin. The Bible is clear on that point. But in our society, it is seen that way less and less. The so-called sexual revolution has eaten away at the traditional standards of morality and self-control among our young people.

But the moral decline is more than just a problem of the young. To a large extent their behavior merely echoes the continuing relaxation of our adult codes of sexual behavior. At the very time in their lives when teens must contend with intense, awakening sexual feelings, they are surrounded by adults who are playing at sex. Indeed, young people are bombarded by sexual stimuli on TV, in books and magazines, in the music they hear, and in the movies they see.

Agonizing Decisions

You ask Stephanie if she is certain that she is pregnant.

"Yes," Mrs. Simpson answers for her. "She had a pregnancy test at Planned Parenthood this morning and it came back positive."

"What's done is done," she continues flatly. "The problem now is to decide what we're going to do about it. I don't think we have much choice. Stephanie will have to get an abortion."

Suddenly Stephanie comes to life. "I can't do that!" she cries. "I can't kill my own baby! How can you ask me to, Mother?"

One of the most agonizing decisions a young woman can be asked to make is what to do with an unplanned, unwanted pregnancy. That decision should be made only after a thorough, careful, and prayerful exploration of all the options. Basically these options are abortion, marriage, single parenthood, foster care, or freeing the baby for adoption.

"How can you even suggest abortion to me?" Stephanie demands again. "You've always been so against it. You said it was a sin! You said it was murder!"

"I am against abortion!" Mrs. Simpson insists. "Too many people nowadays use it as a form of birth control, and I think that is unconscionable. But your situation is different, Stephanie. I mean, you have your education to think about, and your career goals—your whole life. Having that baby will ruin it all!"

It's amazing how many people who claim they do not believe in abortion choose abortion when faced with pregnancy or the pregnancy of someone close. They rationalize their decision by saying that it is the best course of action—just this one time.

For practically everyone the subject of abortion is a sensitive one, charged with emotion. Many understand it to be a moral and spiritual issue as well, which it is. Undoubtedly you have your own strongly held opinions and convictions. You cannot advise someone to do something you consider wrong. Neither can you require that a counselee do something contrary to her own conscience. You can influence, you can advise, and you can offer alternatives, but *you* must not make the final decision.

"I don't think I want to marry my boyfriend," Stephanie volunteers. "At least, not right away. Even if I did, I'm not sure he would want to marry me."

Not too many years ago the solution to Stephanie's problem would have been a "shotgun wedding," and neither she nor her boyfriend would have had a lot to say about it. It was generally accepted that a pregnant girl's father had the right to force the boy involved to marry his daughter. It was up to the young couple to make the best of married life.

As unpleasant as the other options may be, pregnancy must never be the primary reason for marriage. In the best of situations, marriage is a big step that involves a great deal of adjustment, work, and commitment from both partners. But the forced marriage of teenagers "in trouble" is far from the best of situations. Such marriages begin under great strain. Suffering from disillusionment, financial problems, and frustrated dreams and hopes, both partners are sure to feel tied down and soon long for their freedom. Their frustration inevitably turns to resentment. Few of these marriages succeed.

It's Hard Being a Mother

"I know two girls who had babies and decided to keep them," Stephanie continues. "One I never see, but the other one brings her baby to school once in a while, and I sometimes see her downtown. Her little boy is a couple of months old now, and he's so cute! The two of them seem to be doing fine."

Each of the 600,000 girls between the ages of ten and eighteen who give birth to babies each year has to decide whether to keep the baby, to place it in a foster home, or to give it up for adoption. Many of these child-mothers are now deciding to keep and raise their babies.

For some of these girls, the pregnancy was no accident. They actually *wanted* to have babies. In the eyes of many lonely young women, having a baby gives validation to their "grown-up woman" status and proves that they deserve adult respect. They fantasize about a rosy future in which, free of the constraints of school, they can stay at home with nothing to do but care for their babies. They look to these infants to give them the love they crave and to fill a void in their lives.

But babies don't give, they take. As one sixteen-year-old mother put it, too many teens look on parenthood as "playing Mommy." They just don't understand what motherhood is all about. They don't realize that babies cry—sometimes all night—that they get sick, that they are stubborn and uncooperative and demanding.

It's hard being a mother. Being a teenage mother—one who herself hasn't yet reached physical, psychological, or spiritual maturity—is the hardest of all. Under the hard facts of reality, the "happy-ever-after" fantasy usually ends before the baby's first birthday. By then, taking care of and paying the bills for the child has become a crushing burden. Life at home is confining and often unpleasant, especially if the mother is living alone with no companionship but the baby, or with a grandmother who is trying to impose her own standards of child-raising. Even worse, the young mother has not gotten the love she expected from her baby. Faced with these hardships and disappointments, many lose interest in the whole idea of motherhood.

"I want one thing clear right from the start," Mrs. Simpson says to her daughter. "If you decide to go through with this pregnancy, you cannot stay in our house. If your father and I allowed you to remain with the family as if everything was just fine, it would be like us putting a stamp of approval on what you have done. Besides, you would be a terrible role model for your little sisters."

Stephanie stares at her mother. "You mean you'd make me leave home?" she asks.

Leaving home may be the best plan for Stephanie, as it is for many pregnant girls. Wracked by guilt and shame, and holding their daughter responsible for their anguish, some parents cannot give their pregnant daughters the emotional support they need. For other girls, leaving home is their own choice. The stigma and embarrassment of their advancing pregnancy make it more comfortable to live elsewhere.

"Where would I go?" Stephanie asks.

You explain that there are several options to remaining at home. You ask about family friends or relatives who might be willing to allow her to live with them. You suggest that she visit some of the available homes for unwed mothers. You also mention the possibility of staying with a caring Christian family, for many are making room in their homes for girls like Stephanie.

Adoption

After a pause you ask Stephanie if she has considered the possibility of placing the baby for adoption.

It is sad that so much social pressure is put on teenage girls to keep their babies when thousands of childless couples are longing to provide a little one with the advantage of a secure, loving, happy home.

"I don't know," Stephanie says thoughtfully. "I'm not sure I could just say goodby to my baby and give it away with no idea where it will be raised or who its parents will be or what kind of home it will have. If it's my baby, its well-being should be my responsibility."

You tell Stephanie that adoption procedures have changed in recent years. Now, through private adoption, mothers can have a great deal of say in the choice of an adoptive family. Helped by a lawyer who specializes in independent adoptions, Stephanie can look over different applications. From their photographs and information about their backgrounds—including special interests, parenting goals, and spiritual convictions—she can choose the ones she wants to parent her child.

You assure Stephanie that, should she decide on adoption, it will in no way indicate a lack of love for the baby. The opposite is true. A mother who frees her baby for adoption does so because she loves her child enough to want the best possible life for her little one.

Of course, adoption procedures vary from state to state. Should Stephanie decide on this option, she will have to hire an attorney who can advise her on the laws in her own state and the specific procedures for initiating adoption proceedings.

"Do I have to make up my mind ahead of time?" Stephanie asks. "Couldn't I get to know the baby first and see how things go before I decide?"

You tell Stephanie that although it is her legal right to wait, for the good of everyone involved she should make the decision before the baby is born.

"But what if I'm just not sure?" she insists.

Some girls choose to put their babies into foster care, you tell her. This provides extra time to think things out, time to make living arrangements and find a job, time to get life a bit more settled. When she is ready she can bring her baby home to live with her. Or, if she decides that she really isn't able to provide the home her baby needs, she can go ahead and sign the necessary papers relinquishing it for adoption.

But, you warn, there can be problems with foster care. Not all babies are given the love and attention they need. Also, many experts are concerned about the emotional effects of moving a baby from home to home. But the greatest concern of all is that too often babies end up neither living with their mothers nor freed for adoption. Doomed to grow up in the foster care system, which is at best unstable and at worst abusive and dehumanizing, these children find it almost impossible to form the relationships and family bonds so important to healthy development.

Seeking Hope for the Future

Stephanie and her mother have fallen silent. The pressure of the situation is obvious, and so is the strain between the two. You ask Mrs. Simpson if she would mind allowing you to spend some time alone with Stephanie. She agrees and goes outside to wait.

You ask Stephanie how she is feeling about everything.

"Confused," she says. "And scared. Angry, too." After a minute she adds, "And ashamed and guilty. The hardest thing I ever had to do was to tell my parents about this. I know I have betrayed them. I've also betrayed myself. My mother really wants me to have an abortion. I don't want to cause her any more pain than I already have, but I just don't think I can go through with that. I mean, abortion is killing something alive. Still, I just don't know." Her voice trails off into silence.

For a pregnant teenager, life can be a horror. Friends desert her. Suddenly she is no longer one of the crowd. Her emotional mood swings can be wild and unpredictable. And what about the prospects for the rest of her life? Will a decent guy ever want to marry her? Will her family hold this against her forever? And what about God—will He ever forgive her sin?

"If I keep the baby, I know I can't ever go back home to live," she says sadly. "I don't want it to be that way. If only my mom could be a little more understanding. But I guess that's asking too much.

"My parents always felt that sex was an unmentionable subject. I never asked them anything about it because it was obvious that it made them uncomfortable. Of course I knew they considered sex outside of marriage a sin, but that's about all I knew.

"I told my friend Linda about the baby. She says I was really stupid for not using birth control. But the thing is, I never intended to do anything. It just happened. Only bad girls plan ahead."

You tell Stephanie that you agree with Linda in part: the best answer to this predicament is not to get pregnant in the first place. As for birth control, by far the best forms are self-control and abstinence.

With tears glistening in her eyes, Stephanie looks at you imploringly. "It's too late for that," she says. "The question is, what am I going to do now?"

First of all you assure Stephanie that God is ready and willing to forgive her. And although He never promised to take away the consequences of our sin, He has promised that He will never, ever leave us or forsake us. You suggest that the two of you take time to pray together, to ask God's forgiveness, then to ask for His help and guidance in this most important decision.

After the prayer you assure Stephanie that her mother means well in the advice she is giving. So does her friend Linda. But you also remind her that not all the advice she gets will be helpful or unbiased. Often others' recommendations are based on how a decision will affect them.

Although you admit that your advice may have the same limitations, you tell Stephanie that a few facts are especially important for her to keep in mind when considering her options. If she is leaning toward keeping her baby, you tell her, it is important that she explore her reasons for wanting to do so. Is there something in her life that she thinks the baby will make up for? That reason's not good enough. You also caution her about the importance of staying in school. Many communities now have programs at local high schools that allow expectant teens to continue their studies. Those that don't are usually willing to make arrangements to help a girl complete her education.

You tell Stephanie that the final decision is up to her, and you really mean it. It isn't up to her mother and it isn't up to you. You urge Stephanie to listen to all the possibilities and to everyone's opinion with an open mind, and you caution her to be sure that she understands the consequences of each. Then you tell her to spend time alone with the Lord, asking for His wisdom to make the right decision—a decision that she won't regret later.

"Will you talk to my mom?" Stephanie asks. "It's awfully hard for me to talk to her. Maybe you can help her to understand, to stop being so angry with me."

You say you will be happy to try. You call Mrs. Simpson back in. Stephanie chooses to wait outside.

The Question of Sex Education

"How could this have happened to my daughter?" Mrs. Simpson demands. "Did she give you any explanation? She was raised in a good Christian family, you know. Her father and I taught her right from wrong. We were *good* parents! What went wrong?"

You assure Mrs. Simpson that she is in no way to blame for Stephanie's sexual behavior. You add that teenage pregnancy is no longer limited to "bad girls" raised by parents who don't care. Stephanie is typical of a new breed of teenage mothers—daughters of good, hardworking, dedicated parents—yes, even Christian parents. You tell her that the pressures on young people today are very great indeed. Yet Stephanie, like any individual, is ultimately responsible for the behavior choices she makes.

"You know something funny?" Mrs. Simpson says ruefully. "I have always been opposed to sex education in school. I was sure that it would give the kids ideas and make them want to experiment. When it was a required class, I had Stephanie excused from participating. Well, it looks as if she got ideas in spite of me."

The idea that sex education gives adolescents ideas is unrealistic. Young people need to be informed, and parents can be more helpful than anyone else in presenting sexual information in a comfortable and natural manner—if they are willing and able to do so. Unfortunately, many parents find the subject too sensitive to discuss with their children.

With some embarrassment Mrs. Simpson explains, "Her father and I never wanted Stephanie to think that we approved of premarital sex."

Talking about sex with one's children in no way implies permission for them to use what they have learned. Parents should know that even in the absence of moral or religious teachings, knowledgeable teenagers tend to delay sexual experimentation. Furthermore, it is important that parents express their own opinions and convictions about the circumstances under which sex is appropriate. Most teenagers expect their parents to have an opinion on the matter and need to hear both their thoughts and the reasons for them.

Our lives are not value-free, nor do most teenagers want theirs to be. They desperately need to know that they can say no to sex. If children are to be helped to choose a way of loving and caring that is less catastrophic, less painful, and less damaging, they must be given

132

values and standards to live up to. They must know that to be a parent at thirteen or fifteen or seventeen is not an acceptable way to develop a relationship, nor is it an acceptable way to show love or respect for another person. It certainly is not God's way.

You acknowledge the conflicting and painful emotions Mrs. Simpson is experiencing. But you remind her that this is an even worse time for Stephanie, for she is probably facing the most difficult decisions of her entire life. You tell her that her daughter desperately needs every bit of love and support that she and her husband can muster. And you remind Mrs. Simpson that while she obviously has the right to express her opinions, the final decisions rest with Stephanie.

Before Stephanie and her mother leave, you spend time in prayer with them, asking for God's wisdom, strength, and healing power.

A QUICK OVERVIEW

Pregnancy among unwed mothers, especially teenagers, is an especially sensitive situation, and it is difficult for many Christian workers to respond to it objectively. It is easy to condemn the sin that led to the crisis, but much harder to put that issue aside and deal with the question of where to go from here.

Basically the options the woman will consider are these: (1) to end her pregnancy by abortion; (2) to get married; (3) to raise her baby alone; (4) to put the baby into foster care; or (5) to free it for adoption. Regardless of your personal opinion, you must resist the temptation to make this decision for her. Discuss the options, stress the conditions and values you deem important, and tell her why you feel the way you do. Then allow her to make the final decision. Your job is to see that her decision is an informed one that considers both the larger moral issues and achieves a resolution of her own situation.

DOS AND DON'TS

Pregnancy is a crisis situation in that medical care and emotional support must begin early. It is important that the mother-to-be is informed as soon as possible about the options open to her. The decision she makes has consequences that will affect her for the rest of her life.

Do ...

- Encourage the girl to get a pregnancy test. If she only suspects that she is pregnant, encourage her to be tested immediately. Assure her that, whatever the outcome, she is much better off knowing for sure.
- Discuss the options available to her: abortion, marriage, single parenthood, foster care, adoption.
- Make sure that she understands the consequences of each option.
- Encourage her to seek God's wisdom when considering her options.
- Urge her, in making her decision, to put the welfare of her child first.
- Encourage her not to wait until the baby is born and placed in her arms to decide what to do.
- Emphasize that, if she wants to keep her baby, she should explore her reasons for wanting to do so.
- Help her to see realistically what is involved in raising a child. Help her to assess carefully her ability to cope with all the ramifications of motherhood.
- Encourage her to seek counseling with someone who can help her through the difficult months ahead.
- Encourage her, if she decides to release the baby for adoption, to stipulate that it be placed in a Christian home.
- All you can to help her arrange to stay in school. Even if there is no special program for pregnant teens locally, most schools will cooperate in making the necessary arrangement.
- Encourage her to start planning now how to avoid an unwanted pregnancy in the future.
- Pray together with the girl, and with her parents, if possible.
- Let her know that this is not the end of her life. Give her Philippians 3:13–14 to claim for her own: ". . . But one thing I do: Forgetting what is behind and straining toward what is ahead, I press on toward the goal to win the prize for which God has called me heavenward in Christ Jesus" (NIV).

Don't ...

- Take sides when there is friction between the girl and her parents.
- Dismiss the sin that has caused the problem, but don't dwell

on it either. The important point now is where to go from here.

- Attempt to answer medical questions or give medical advice.
- Try to force the girl into taking action that she adamantly resists, even though it may seem to you to offer the best solution. Remember, the decision *must* be hers.
- Attempt to answer legal questions concerning adoption, foster care, or other subjects. The laws vary widely among states and communities. Leave the legal advice to attorneys.
- Give her the idea that any of the options will bring an easy resolution of her problem. None will. There are no easy answers for her.

RESOURCES

Hotlines:

Bethany Christian Services: 1–800–238–4269

Family Life Services: 1–800–368–3336

National Adoption Hotline: 202–463–7563

National Pregnancy Hotline

1–800–344–7211
1–800–831–5881 (in California)

A facility operated by Family Life Federation, a pro-life group, which will provide counseling on options other than abortion and refer the caller to local organizations.

The Child Welfare League of America. For a list of local services, send a request accompanied by a stamped, self-addressed envelope to the following address:

67 Irving Place
New York, NY 10003

The following organizations have offices across the country. You can obtain information about their services by telephone.

Bethany Christian Services. Bethany offers a full range of child-placement, counseling, and adoption services; temporary foster care; shepherding home care; and limited group home placement.

901 Eastern Avenue N.E.
Grand Rapids, MI 49503
(616) 459–6273

Canadian Birthright Centers. For services offered, see Bethany Christian Services.

National Office
777 Coxwell Avenue
Toronto, Ontario M4C3C6
(416) 469–1111

Crisis Pregnancy Centers of the Christian Action Council. This is the nation's largest Protestant pro-life group. There are sixty CPC centers to date, each directed and sponsored by a local church. Services include free pregnancy tests, counseling, a slide presentation explaining fetal development and the abortion process, housing in Christian homes, transportation to medical facilities, and maternity clothes and baby supplies.

Christian Action Council
422 C Street N.E.
Washington, DC 20002
(202) 544–1720

Evangelical Child and Family Agency. This group's services include professional counseling, housing, medical care, and financial planning. No fees are charged for counseling unmarried parents.

1530 North Main Street
Wheaton, IL 60187
(312) 653–6400

National Committee for Adoption

(202) 463–7563

For additional information on services for pregnant teens and their options, write:

The National Organization on Adolescent Pregnancy and Parenting (NOAPP)

521 West Fourth Street
Fort Worth, TX 76102

Sex Education Resources

American Academy of Pediatrics
Department L
1801 Hinman Avenue
Evanston, IL 60210
(800) 323–0797

National Clearinghouse for Family Planning Information

P.O. Box 2225
Rockville, MD 20852
(301) 881–9400

Planned Parenthood Federation of America

810 Seventh Avenue
New York, NY 10010
(212) 541–7800

Sex Information and Education Council of the United States

80 Fifth Avenue, Suite 801
New York, NY 10011
(212) 929–2300

SUGGESTED READING

Bell, Ruth. *Changing Bodies/Changing Lives*. New York: Random House, 1981.
Jefferson, John, *Abortion and the Christian*, Phillipsburg, N.J.: Presbyterian and Reformed, 1984.
McGuire, Paula. *It Won't Happen to Me: Teenagers Talk About Pregnancy*. New York: Delacorte Press, 1983.
O'Brien, Bev. *Mom . . . I'm Pregnant*. Wheaton: Tyndale House, 1982.
Roggow, Linda, and Carolyn Owens. *Handbook for Pregnant Teenagers*. Grand Rapids: Zondervan, 1985.

A guide to decision making, describing the resources and social agencies that can offer essential help. Strong anti-abortion stand.

Short, Ray E. *Sex, Dating and Love*. Minneapolis: Augsburg, 1984.

Answers to seventy-seven frequently asked questions on dating, love, marriage, relationships, and sex, with biblical basis.

Strom, Kay Marshall. *Chosen Families*. Grand Rapids: Zondervan, 1985.

The options open in adoption, with a section on private adoptions plus a number of references.

137

U.S. Dept. of Health, Education and Welfare. *Teenage Pregnancy: Everybody's Problem.* Consumer Information Center, Dept. 087F, Pueblo, CO 81009. Cost: $1.

Young, Curt. *The Least of These: What Everyone Should Know About Abortion.* Chicago: Moody Press, 1984.

Zimmerman, Martha. *Should I Keep My Baby?* Minneapolis: Bethany House, 1983.

> Good advice on a wide range of decisions facing unwed, expectant mothers. Takes a strong stand against abortion.

LOCAL REFERENCES

OBSTETRICIANS

The first thing a pregnant girl needs is good prenatal care. Without it many end up with serious physical deficiencies such as malnutrition, anemia, and high blood pressure. This is vital for her own well-being and for her child's.

NAME:

Number:

Notes:

NAME:

Number:

Notes:

LOCAL ADOPTION AGENCY

Contact Person:

Number:

ATTORNEY

Preferably one who specializes in private adoptions:

138

NAME:

Number:

Notes:

PREGNANCY COUNSELING ORGANIZATIONS

There are many of these around the country, some of which are listed in this chapter under the heading "Resources." These organizations are prepared to provide professional advice and information.

NAME:

Number:

Contact Person:

Notes:

NAME:

Number:

Contact Person:

Notes:

PLANNED PARENTHOOD
Number:

Contact Person:

Notes:

CATHOLIC FAMILY AGENCY

Number:

Contact Person:

Notes:

COMPREHENSIVE ADOLESCENT PREGNANCY CENTERS

There are a number of these in cities across the United States. These centers offer medical, educational, ethical, and social services designed exclusively to meet the needs of the parents.

NAME:

Number:

Contact Person:

Notes:

OTHER RESOURCES

NAME:

Number:

Contact Person:

Notes:

NAME:

Number:

Contact Person:

Notes:

HOW CAN THE CHRISTIAN COMMUNITY HELP?

Prevention is the best solution to the problem of unwanted pregnancy. But the likelihood of prevention is diminished by Christians who insist on burying their heads in the sand. The problem cannot be solved until girls are reached *before* they become pregnant.

Too often our society and its institutions pride themselves on being value-free. This attitude forces adolescents to look to each other for a basis for decision making, and this often leads them to the wrong conclusions. Christians must counter this with the truth that our lives are *not* value-free. Values have been established by God Himself. We must give young people the opportunity to examine our values, to question, understand, and share them.

Encourage teenagers and adults to talk together so that they can discover what beliefs and principles they share. This will also allow teens to define their own values and to affirm and live by them.

Many church denominations and Christian groups are helping to arrange housing options for pregnant teens—Adventists, Catholic Family Services, Lutheran Social Services, the Salvation Army, and Birthright, to name a few. This can be done on a local level as well. Rather than establishing larger group homes, a church may recruit volunteer families who will offer a room in their own homes.

Another service that Christian groups can provide pregnant teens is surrogate mothers to girls whose own parents refuse to stand by them. A web of friendly, supportive relationships surrounding the girls allows them to feel secure while they make plans for the future.

Churches can also provide space for socializing and training pregnant teens in matters of schooling, jobs, health, baby care, and training in parenting. They should include a strong emphasis on self-control and abstinence, the two most effective and least discussed methods of birth control. There should also be sound teaching on the love and forgiveness of God.

10.   *Wife Abuse*

It is six o'clock on a Friday evening. Anxious to lock up the office and get home for dinner, you groan when you hear a knock at the door. You open it to admit a sobbing woman who is battered and bruised. She pours out an incredible story of torment and abuse at the hands of her husband.

Each year millions of women are hospitalized with injuries that could only be caused by beatings. According to the FBI, during one year alone 40 percent of the women killed were murdered by their husbands. Although most cases of wife battering are never reported, authorities estimate that fully half of all American wives will be physically abused by their partners sometime during their marriages. A foremost group of research sociologists tells us that in today's American family, violence is probably as common as love.

Wife abuse presents counselors with a complex, frightening, frustrating situation. Even defining the term is a problem. Does it apply to a woman who is pushed around or slapped by her husband during a heated argument? How about a wife whose sarcastic taunts provoke a fight that ends in her being beaten senseless? What about a woman who is never struck physically but suffers verbal and emotional abuse?

Although nonphysical abuse such as humiliation, verbal attacks, and harassment can be terribly painful and damaging, it is not likely to be life threatening. These situations can best be handled by professional counselors who are trained to deal with them. But physical abuse is quite another thing; it can quickly become a matter of life and death. For our purposes, then, wife abuse can be defined as a man's use of physical violence against his wife with the intention of producing bodily injury.

A Common Problem

The bruised, sobbing woman who sits before you could be of any age, race, or nationality. She might live in an inner-city tenement, a middle-class tract house, or a luxurious hilltop mansion. Her battering husband could be a doctor, a policeman, a welfare recipient, a professor, a plumber, a clergyman. No segment of our society—no race, religion, profession, or socioeconomic group—is exempt.

"No one would believe what my husband does to me," the anguished woman tells you. "People who know him think he's a great guy. And in some ways he really is."

Contrary to popular belief, most batterers are not "crazy" psychotics. Except for the inability to control their aggressive impulses, the majority lead fairly normal lives. Their common problem is that they have learned to deal with anger and frustration through violence.

Certain characteristics seem to predispose these men to violent behavior. Many were raised in an atmosphere of violence, the victims of child abuse or beatings. Most suffer from low self-esteem and insecurity. Despite nagging doubts about their masculinity, most are overly concerned with living up to a tough, macho role. Possessive and jealous, many batterers can be charming and loving when they want to be. Some are successful, highly respected leaders in their communities and churches. Because they are so good at hiding their abusive side, few outsiders suspect what they are like in the privacy of their homes.

"I just knew he was going to start in on me because he'd been drinking all day," the woman continues. "He can't control himself when he drinks."

Alcohol is often blamed for a man's violence against his wife. While there is a correlation between the two, alcohol cannot necessarily be considered the cause of the beatings. Drinking lowers a person's control and inhibitions, but it does not cause the tendencies toward violence. Many experts believe that batterers use drinking as a convenient excuse for their behavior, an excuse many wives are willing to accept.

A Three-Phase Pattern

"During the past week or so he's been increasingly irritable," relates the woman. "When he gets this way I can't do anything right. No matter how I clean the house, it isn't clean enough to suit him. Whatever I cook, it isn't what he wants. When this starts, I know it's just a matter of time before I get beaten. But tomorrow will be another story. He'll be home early with a bouquet of roses—all hugs and kisses and promises. That's how it always is."

Most cases of continuing wife battering follow a familiar three-phase pattern: the tension-building phase, the actual beating, and the loving respite phase. In the first phase tension builds over a series of occurrences and minor irritations. The wife, seeing trouble coming, does everything in her power to keep the peace. But her cowering compliance only seems to infuriate her husband further.

When the mounting tension reaches a certain point, abuse is inevitable. Knowing this, some women seem to provoke their husbands deliberately "just to get it over with." The actual beating may be triggered by something quite trivial. One woman was stomped to death by her husband because the car wouldn't start and she was unable to pick up his cleaning. One husband broke his wife's arm because he didn't like the tablecloth she put on the table.

In many instances, when the beating is over, the batterer is genuinely sorry for what he has done. Apologetic, charming, and loving, he vows in total sincerity that he will never again hurt his wife. And at the time he honestly believes he can keep his promises. Though his wife has heard it all before, she so badly wants it to be true that she is willing to try "just one more time." Before long, however, the tension builds and the cycle is repeated. Once this vicious cycle of violence begins, few couples are able to stop it. And despite the best-intentioned promises and resolutions, it never will end without professional help.

"Our children are still at home with my husband," the woman tells you, "but I'm sure they are all right. He talks rough, but he has never laid a hand on them. If he ever did hurt those kids, I'd take them and leave in a minute!"

Apparently her children are not being abused. But many youngsters who live in this kind of home are abused—if not by their violent fathers, then by their angry, frustrated mothers. Even if they aren't harmed physically, they are seldom able to avoid emotional injuries. Anxiety, terror, depression, nervousness, and distrust are symptoms commonly found among children raised in violent families. Even more frightening are statistics which indicate that children who learn firsthand the lessons of abuse are likely to become the abusers of the future. Domestic violence, it seems, is a learned behavior, frequently passed from one generation to the next.

The devastating impact of domestic violence touches every one of us. It has been said that violence in the streets begins at home, and the statistics seem to bear this out. Studies indicate that as many as 90 percent of incarcerated violent offenders were themselves victims of violent homes.

Bound to Stay

"We had only been married for a month when he first hit me," the woman continues. "He was angry because I left the door unlocked when I went to the store. He said if I was going to behave like a child he would have to punish me like a child. It was just a slap across the face that time, but over the years his attacks have gotten progressively worse. Today I thought he was going to kill me!"

Herein lies the paradox: battered wives live a nightmare, yet many never attempt to leave their husbands. Furthermore, most who do leave soon return. Why do so many women stay in abusive situations? This can partially be explained by what is known as "learned helplessness." Feeling that she can do nothing to help herself, that there are no options open to her, a victim of abuse may simply stop resisting and passively accept the violence as a way of life. The longer she puts up with the abuse, the less she likes herself. Feeling more and more a failure, she feels more and more trapped and powerless.

Many abused wives are bound to their husbands by fear. Threats such as "I'll find you and kill you" or "If you leave me I'll kill myself" are common. Other women stay for economic reasons. What's a woman to do if she has no money, no job, and no place to go? Still others stay out of guilt. Feeling responsible for her husband's violence, certain that she provoked him to it, the guilt-ridden woman places the blame on herself instead of on her husband, where it belongs.

"I don't want to be responsible for breaking up my marriage," the woman tells you. "If I can just be the wife he wants me to be, I'm sure he won't hit me anymore."

Besides feeling a strong sense of responsibility to their spouses and families, many women stay in the hope of changing their husbands, of somehow stopping the violent outbursts. But regardless of what she does, unless the wife leaves or the batterer gets help, the beatings are almost certain to continue and to increase in frequency and intensity. The idea that an abused wife can change her husband is both unrealistic and dangerous.

Many Christian wives also feel a spiritual responsibility for their non-Christian husbands. Convinced that if the abuser would only become a Christian the problem would be solved, the determination of these women to "save" their men is praised and encouraged by many in the Christian community. But saving and changing people is

God's responsibility, which He can accomplish without the woman having to live in danger.

"According to my husband, if I'd be submissive like the Bible says I should, there wouldn't be a problem," the woman tells you. "I try to be submissive, I really do. What am I doing wrong?"

Attempting to understand the biblical teaching on submission and how it applies to them frequently leaves Christian abuse victims confused and frustrated. The problem is compounded by churches and individuals who emphasize submission to the extreme. The result is that many battered wives find it impossible to break away from their strict views even when their lives are at risk.

Abusive men love the term "submission" because it enables them to justify their violent actions. Piously they quote Scripture passages such as God's words to Eve: "He shall rule over thee" (Genesis 3:16). Or the Pauline admonition: "Wives, submit yourselves unto your own husbands" (Ephesians 5:22). Or 1 Corinthians 7:4: "The wife's body does not belong to her alone, but also to her husband."

It is vital that biblical teachings concerning submission be balanced with what the Bible has to say about human worth and the sanctity of life. It is important, too, that traditional biases not be confused with scriptural truths.

Force and violence have no place in a marriage. To be successful, marriage must be a partnership in which each submits to the other, builds each other up, and recognizes Christ as the head of their home.

What Is the Way Out?

"I don't know if I can take it any more," the woman says in a strained voice. "I'm confused, scared. I believe that marriage is a lifelong arrangement. In my wedding vows I said, 'For better or for worse, till death do us part.' But does that mean I have to stay with my husband until he kills me?"

That's a good question. Many Christians believe that divorce is unacceptable under any circumstances. Whatever our personal convictions, we as counselors must be very careful in giving advice. To admonish a battered wife to stay and work out her marriage as best she can is inviting disaster.

Staying around for the next beating or getting a divorce are not the only options open to a battered wife. She can move out

147

temporarily with the understanding that she will return only when her husband demonstrates a true determination to change. This includes accepting the responsibility for his actions, voluntarily entering a counseling program, and participating in a written agreement stating specifically what action will be taken should the violence recur.

"How can my husband get away with this?" the woman demands in exasperation. "If it was anyone else he was hitting, he'd be in jail!"

Wife abuse is a felony in all fifty states, but the law often fails to protect battered wives satisfactorily. Because the police, the courts, and social agencies traditionally support the sanctity and privacy of the home, they are reluctant to interfere in domestic affairs. Yet it is possible to use existing laws to offer some degree of protection to abuse victims.

"One person tells me one thing, someone else tells me something else," the woman tells you. "What is the best thing for a battered wife to do?"

As with most complex problems, there is no single right answer. The correct course of action is different in the case of a wildly irrational man who threatens to murder his wife from that of a contrite man who admits his problem and asks for help.

It is important that the abuse victim be guided into a careful and realistic assessment of her situation. If the abuse she suffers is frequent enough or severe enough, or if her life has been threatened, she must get out of the home immediately. In fact, leaving may well be the only thing that can save her marriage. In many cases it is the wife's leaving that finally forces an abuser to admit his problem and seek help. As long as she stays, he has no reason to change.

Until she finds a place of safety where she can think clearly, a battered wife cannot really explore her options. For this reason, our greatest concern as counselors should be to get the woman to a haven.

The Abused Wife's Options

As counselors we can support and comfort and guide and advise, but we must not determine the ultimate course of action that an abused wife will take. She alone can do that. Here are the most likely decisions she will face and the implications of each:

1. The abuse victim who decides to stay in her home without insisting on evidence of a major change is essentially resigning herself to her fate. While this is of course an option, she should clearly understand that it is a dangerous choice. To survive, she must be determined to do anything necessary to avoid upsetting her husband. She should expect no cooperation from him.

It is vitally important that a woman who makes this decision establishes a support system of people on whom she can call in a time of crisis. For her own protection she should hide extra money, car keys, and important documents in a safe but accessible place. She should arrange for a safe place for her and her children to go in an emergency, and she should keep the phone number of the police department handy.

2. The battered woman who decides to stay and commit herself to changing her husband and saving her marriage should understand that she cannot change her spouse. It isn't possible. Furthermore, while she is waiting for the change to happen she will be living in a volatile and dangerous situation that is certain to damage the children who will be witnessing the violence against her.

If the woman feels trapped because of her marriage commitment, she should be reminded that her husband's violent behavior has already violated their marriage covenant. Staying in a dangerous situation when her husband shows no sign of change is no virtue.

3. For the abused woman who decides to leave, locating a safe place for herself and her children to live is the first priority. It is important that she establish a record of the abuse she has suffered while the details of the last episode of violence are still in her mind. This information can be crucial if she should ever decide to file charges.

Leaving the spouse is a very difficult step for most battered wives. For their own mental and emotional health, they should be put in touch with a competent counselor. Besides professional help, she will need supportive encouragement from the Christian community.

4. The wife beater who wants to change must prove his sincerity by immediately getting competent, professional counseling. Without it, he is unlikely to change.

The abuser must be confronted with the reality of what he is doing to himself and his family. He needs to face the seriousness of his actions and accept the responsibility for them. Instead of handling his frustrations through aggression, he must learn to deal with his emotions through acceptable behavior. Only when he understands that it is human to feel anger but inhuman to release those feelings by beating others can he gain respect for himself and his wife.

5. What about the children of violent families, the innocent victims who are helpless to decide their own fate? Is there any help for them? Like their parents, children from violent homes badly need competent counseling. Without it they are likely to perpetuate the abusive behavior they have witnessed.

The goal is to help these children to understand but not accept the problem in their families. They must realize that violence is wrong and has to be stopped. Unless they learn to deal with anger appropriately, they too will grow up to handle their frustration through aggression.

Children raised with violence desperately need healthy modeling and reinforcement. If allowed to spend time in nonviolent homes, these children will see that not all families are like theirs; not all families beat up the ones they profess to love.

A QUICK OVERVIEW

The complex, confusing problem of wife abuse can precipitate a dangerous crisis. Although she is likely to have suffered abuse for years, the battered woman may be reluctant to leave her home for various reasons. The fact that she has sought a counselor indicates that she realizes that the situation is out of control, that it is more than she can handle. It is at this time of crisis that she will be most open to making badly needed changes in her life.

Our first consideration as counselors is to see that the abused woman is sheltered in a safe place. Once out of danger, she should be in contact with a professional who is qualified to present her with her options.

Regardless of our personal convictions on the best course of action for a battered wife, this is a decision that only she can make. While we can and should advise her carefully and sensitively, we must not attempt to coerce her into taking any action against her will. We should be prepared for the following possible decisions: resignation and a decision to stay with her husband, a total commitment to her marriage and to changing him, the decision to leave him.

Should the woman make what seems to you an unwise decision, assure her of your concern and prayerful support and be ready with referrals for the next inevitable crisis.

DOS AND DON'TS

In cases of domestic violence, good advice is essential and bad advice can be deadly. We must be careful that, out of ignorance or oversight, we do not end up doing more harm than good.

Do ...

- Treat the matter seriously. Physical abuse is a matter of life and death.
- Emphasize to the battered woman that she is not to blame for the abuse. No matter what it was that precipitated the attack, she did not deserve to be hit.
- Let her talk. Even though it may not be pleasant to hear what she has to tell, she needs to have someone listen.
- Believe what she says, no matter how unbelievable her story may be.
- Help the woman to see that marriage is not an owner-property arrangement. No husband has ownership rights over his wife, nor does he have the right to use force to control her.
- Be sensitive. Realize that the woman needs support, not condemnation.
- Assure the battered woman that it isn't God's will that she suffer abuse. It is not a divine means of punishing her.
- Let her know that it is possible for her to make changes in her life. Assure her that there are many people who can and will help.
- Determine the frequency and severity of the abuse. If her life has been threatened or if the physical violence has happened before, her life could be at risk and she needs protection. Warn her not to return home.
- Help her find a place of safety to which she can go.
- Encourage her to see a doctor if she has been physically abused. Many abusers, though they claim to be out of control, deliberately inflict injuries in places where they will not be easily seen. It's possible that the woman might be more seriously injured than either of you realize.
- Pray with her. It will calm and comfort her, but also it really does work.
- Assure the wife that leaving home does not necessarily lead to a divorce. Tell her that leaving is often the very thing that causes an abuser to admit the problem and to seek help.

151

- Make sure that the battered woman understands her options. If she decides to return home, she must understand and accept the possible consequences.
- Emphasize that only she can make the decision as to which course of action she will take. You can advise and refer, but she must act.
- Suggest that if she returns home she tell her husband, "Never again! If this does happen again, I will leave you!" It is vital, however, that she not give any ultimatums or threats she is not fully prepared to carry through.
- Stress the necessity of getting through to the offender. Unless he admits the problem and gets help, the abuse will most likely recur. If his wife leaves him, he will probably initiate the same violence in another relationship.
- Assure the woman that you will be available to provide continued support and encouragement to her family and that you will help them to make full use of the available resources.
- Respect and believe in people's capacity to change and grow. With God all things are possible!

Don't ...

- Treat the problem lightly. Domestic violence can be deadly.
- Be condescending. A pat on the shoulder and an assurance that "everything will work out for the best" are no help to a woman who has just been beaten by her husband.
- Offer pat answers or platitudes.
- Discourage her from talking by acting embarrassed or uncomfortable.
- Be chauvinistic. Men do not own their wives, nor do they have a right to discipline them or "keep them in line."
- Blame the abused woman for her predicament. Be careful not even to imply that she may have "asked for it." No one, no matter what she's said or done, deserves to be beaten.
- Accuse her of failing to be submissive to her husband.
- Begin by stressing that she must preserve the family unit at all costs, by quoting biblical texts on the sanctity of marriage or by warning her against divorce. Removing herself from a dangerous situation does not mean the marriage must end.
- Send her home, especially if she has been beaten before or if her life has been threatened. You must not cause her to return to a potentially life-threatening situation.

- Send her to a volunteer home if there is any reason to suspect that her presence might put the family in danger. Be aware of threats against anyone who helps her.
- Advise her to be patient and submissive in the hope that she will lead her husband to the Lord. His salvation is up to God, not her.
- Try to provide more counseling than you are trained to give. Poor advice, even when sincerely given by a well-meaning counselor, is likely to do much more harm than good. Your job is to identify the woman's immediate needs, then to refer her to people who are trained to deal with the problem.
- Advise hitting back. It's an invitation to serious injury.
- Tell her to threaten to leave unless she truly intends to do so and is able to follow through on her threat.
- Give up on her if she ignores your advice and refuses to get help. Let her know that you are interested and concerned. Give her the names and addresses of emergency services, and encourage her to use them when she is ready.

When a woman comes on behalf of someone else, suggest that she . . .

- Let the abused woman know that she is aware of what is happening.
- Assure the battered woman that she is a friend and is willing to listen whenever the victim needs to talk.
- Not downplay the violence. Wife abuse is a serious situation.
- Help the victim to see herself as a valuable, worthwhile person who has the right to be treated with love and respect and to live a nonviolent life.
- Acquaint herself with the resources that are available to battered women and their children, both Christian and secular.
- Not encourage the battered woman to go back home and try to work out the problem.
- Be prepared to help the victim find a safe place to go and, if transportation is a problem, to offer to take her there.
- Not disclose the whereabouts of the battered woman to her husband or to anyone who might tell him.
- Encourage the victim to establish a record of the abuse she has suffered. If medical attention is obtained, the name of the physician or emergency room staff members should be recorded. If the police are called, a report should be filed.

153

- Not encourage the woman to try to reform or reason with the violent man. It almost never works.
- Be patient with the abused wife. It's easy to become frustrated with someone who seemingly refuses to help herself. But remember that many battered wives are emotionally paralyzed and controlled by fear and confusion.

RESOURCES

Emergency Shelter Homes. These are usually the best emergency housing alternative for battered women. Staff members are available as sources of support and are trained in dealing with the problem of family violence. These homes are available in most communities, but they will vary in philosophy, the space available, and their house rules (how long a woman can stay, whether or not children are accepted, etc.). For the protection of the women staying there, the location of these homes is usually a strictly guarded secret. Access is available through hotlines, the police department, and community health centers. Organizations that can provide contacts for such shelter are listed later in this section.

Hotel/Motel Shelters. These are less to be preferred than emergency shelter homes. Women sheltered here tend to feel isolated and depressed. If this is the only alternative, someone should stay in frequent contact with the woman to encourage and support her and to help her with any needs that might arise.

Safe Homes. Private residences where abused women are sheltered can be set up through the community or the church. Safe-home volunteers should have training in the special needs of the victims of family violence. It must be noted that in some cases there may be potential risk to a volunteer family. It is not appropriate to use such a home if it is known that the victim's husband may pose a danger.

Hotlines. These operate in many communities and can be a valuable source of help and guidance.

Mental Health Agency. Services include crisis counseling as well as individual, marital, child, family, and group counseling.

Social Service Agencies. These can provide child protective services, financial assistance, child care, counseling, payment for emergency shelter, and transportation.

Legal Aid Society. Services include consultation regarding rights and advocacy with welfare services.

YWCA. This organization may provide shelter, counseling services and support groups.

Hospital Emergency Rooms. Immediate medical care is available. If such care is sought, a record should be made of the injuries and the names of emergency room personnel involved in the treatment.

The Salvation Army. A Family Service Department works with abused women within the framework of a Christian perspective. It provides shelter for battered women and individual and group counseling for them and their husbands. The staff generally comprises evangelical Christian counselors who are trained in social work and psychology.

The following organizations have information about state contacts and shelters where a battered woman can find help:

Center for Women Policy Studies. This center is funded by the Law Enforcement Assistance Administration to provide technical assistance to anyone involved in domestic violence. It keeps an up-to-date file in its office to advise people where to locate the resources closest to their homes. The address is:

> 2000 P Street, N.W. Suite 508
> Washington, DC 20036
> (202) 872–1770

National Coalition Against Domestic Violence

> 1728 N Street, N.W.
> Washington, DC 20036
> (202) 347–7015

Center for the Prevention of Sexual and Domestic Violence. This interreligious, educational ministry can be a helpful resource for the religious community. It assists clergy, lay counselors, and secular professionals in regard to family violence. The address is:

> 4250 South Mead Street
> Seattle, WA 98118
> (206) 725–1903

Working Together. This is a bimonthly newsletter published by:

The Center for the Prevention of Sexual and
Domestic Violence
1914 North 34th Street
Suite 205
Seattle, WA 98103
(206) 634–1903

Emerge. A counseling service for abusive men, Emerge offers
both information and materials.

25 Huntington Avenue
Boston, MA 02116
(617) 267–7690

Women Against Violence Emergency Services (WAVES). This group
makes referrals to local shelters.

P.O. Box 1121
Berkeley, CA 94701
(415) 527–HELP

Betsy Warrior. For $3.50 Ms. Warrior will send a directory of
shelter and services for battered women. Contact her at:

45 Pleasant Street
Cambridge, MA 02139

SUGGESTED READING

Because the majority of the secular material on this subject is
written from a strong feminist bias, it has come under a great deal of
criticism from the Christian community. This literature makes some
valid points, but on the negative side it also treats marriage as
dispensable, degrades the role of homemaker for a wife, and tends to
blame Christianity for women's problems.

Furthermore, the crucial issues of separation and divorce, family
authority and responsibility, the meaning of suffering, and the
possibility of forgiveness are seldom addressed in secular material.

Before recommending books, become familiar with them. Even if
you do not read them all completely, be aware of each author's
perspective, especially on issues that have special concern for
Christians.

Barnett, Ellen R., Carla B. Pittman, Cynthia K. Ragan, and Marsha K.
Salus. *Family Violence: Intervention Strategies.* Washington: U.S. Dept. of
Health and Human Services, 1980.

Fortune, Marie M. *Sexual Violence: The Unmentionable Sin*. New York: Pilgrim, 1983.

Written by a Protestant minister who has worked for several years with the Center for the Prevention of Sexual and Domestic Violence. Devotes second half to practical strategies for Christian ministers in dealing with victims of domestic violence, rape, and child molestation. Includes how to deal with wife beaters, molesters, and rapists.

Fortune, Marie, and Denise Hormann. *Family Violence: A Workshop Manual for Clergy and Other Service*. Seattle: Center for the Prevention of Sexual and Domestic Violence, 1980.

Green, Holly Wagner. *Turning Fear to Hope*. Nashville: Thomas Nelson, 1984.

Lovett, C. S. *The Compassionate Side of Divorce*. Baldwin Park, Calif.: Personal Christianity, 1978.

Martin, Del. *Battered Wives*. San Francisco: Glide Publications, 1976.

Written from a secular point of view.

Straus, Murray A., Richard J. Gelles, and Suzanne K. Steinmetz. *Behind Closed Doors: Violence in the American Family*. New York: Doubleday Anchor, 1980.

Strom, Kay Marshall. *A Question of Submission: A Painful Look at Wife Battering*. Portland, Ore.: Multnomah Press, 1986.

Walker, Lenore. *The Battered Woman*. New York: Harper & Row, 1979.

A pioneer in writing on the subject of wife abuse. A secular book.

LOCAL REFERENCES

HOTLINE

Obtain this number from your telephone directory or the police department.

NUMBER:

Notes:

You will need an up-to-date list of competent professionals, preferably experienced in dealing with wife abuse.

PSYCHIATRIST OR PSYCHOLOGIST

NAME:

Number:

Notes:

MEDICAL DOCTOR

NAME:

Number:

Notes:

FAMILY COUNSELOR

NAME:

Number:

Notes:

Since your first concern will be to get a battered woman to a place of safety, be sure you have at least one number available for immediate shelter. It is better to have several choices to meet a variety of situations.

EMERGENCY SHELTER HOME

Number:

Contact Person:

Notes:

OTHER PLACES OF REFUGE

NAME:

Number:

Notes:

NAME:

Number:

Notes:

LOCAL SOCIAL SERVICE, LEGAL AID, AND MENTAL HEALTH AGENCIES

NAME:

Number:

Contact Person:

Notes:

NAME:

Number:

Contact Person:

Notes:

SALVATION ARMY

Number:

Contact Person:

Services Available:

Notes:

OTHER PERSONS AND ORGANIZATIONS HELPFUL IN A CRISIS

NAME:

Number:

Notes:

NAME:

Number:

Notes:

11.   *Why Me?*

"Why me? I'm a good person. I'm a Christian! Why did God let this happen to me?"

It may be Sue, the wife of the unfaithful husband, or Joanne, the adulterous wife, who is pleading for an answer to this question. Or it may be Marilyn, who has become entrapped by alcohol. It may be someone whose family has been shattered by violence or whose teenaged daughter is pregnant. The woman who was attacked and raped will surely ask the question, as will Melody, whose life is so unbearable that she can think of no release but death. In a desperate effort to make some sense of what has happened to her, a woman who came to you for help in a crisis will likely turn to you again for an answer to her greatest question: "Why?"

It is an important question that has been asked throughout history. Why do good people suffer? Where is God's justice? How do the scriptural promises of protection and care fit in?

It may be that the sufferer's problem is a result of her own sin. Has she been unfaithful to her husband? Is she unmarried and pregnant? Her decision to disobey God's laws regarding sexual behavior is the cause of the problem.

Or her suffering may be a direct result of having made a poor decision. Women who have married abusive or alcoholic men are examples of this.

When the suffering is caused by our own actions, whether from sin or from unwise decisions, it is hardly necessary to ask, "Why me?" The answer should be obvious. As counselors we should help the hurting person to understand and accept this. That is not to say that people whose actions have brought about their problems don't deserve our comfort and caring. They do, of course. God is in the business of forgiving. Tell her so!

But what about people who suffer from situations they neither caused nor had the power to prevent? What about victims of rape or incest? What about an adulterer's spouse or the parents of a pregnant or suicidal child? Why would God allow this suffering to come to innocent people?

A Hurting World

We live in a hurting world, and much of the pain is caused by human sinfulness. Sin invariably causes suffering, either to the sinner or to someone else. With rare exceptions, the situations explored in this book are caused by someone's hurtful, sinful actions. No human being is guaranteed protection from the sinfulness of another.

"A friend of mine came awfully close to being assaulted," the woman tells you. "She told me that she prayed and God miraculously rescued her. Well, I prayed too. So why didn't God protect me?"

We all know of times when Christians narrowly escape tragedy. How easy it is to attribute these unhesitatingly to "divine intervention" or "the saving hand of God." While these may be comforting thoughts to some people, they merely add to the pain and anxiety of the woman who was *not* spared a tragedy.

God can and does miraculously intervene in the lives of people sometimes. But He doesn't always. And herein lies the problem with the friend's question, "So why didn't God protect me?" The implication is that those who are not spared are not under God's protective care. What a devastating effect this way of thinking can have on a person already struggling to make some sense of what has happened!

That the friend was spared should be reason for gratitude and thankfulness to God. But it is a mistake to assume that she was rescued simply *because* she prayed or trusted the Lord. God's ways are not so simple.

Many people are convinced that God shouldn't let bad things happen to His children, especially those who seek diligently to serve Him. But this is not what the Scriptures teach, and it definitely is not what we see happening in everyday life. No, God doesn't put a special circle of protection around His children. It was never His intention that they be exempt from pain and suffering.

What, then, are we to do with the many biblical passages that promise the Lord's protective care for His children? By all means continue to use them to comfort those who come to you for counsel. God has promised to stay with His children in all circumstances, to help them through the difficult times. Best of all, He has promised to keep them from separation from Him (Romans 8:37–39). And God *always* keeps His promises. With confidence we can assure a hurting woman that God is still sovereign and He is still on her side.

"Everyone asks me if I have discovered God's purpose for

allowing me to go through this," the woman says with a sigh. "I wish I could say yes, but I can't. They say when I do understand, I'll thank Him for the experience. But I don't think that will ever happen!"

Is it fair to assume that God causes problems and suffering, or even allows them, for a specific purpose? Does He send trials and tragedies to us in order to teach lessons or to bring blessings? It is hard—very hard—to accept horrible experiences such as rape or incest or suicide as having happened for no beneficial reason at all. To explain them, some Christians go to ridiculous lengths to identify the "good reason" behind the bad happenings in life.

God does surely allow us to grow and mature as a result of the bad events that happen to us. He does bring blessings out of those situations; Romans 8:28 assures us of this. But that is not the same as saying that God causes, or even allows, such happenings for this purpose.

"Why do I have to be the one that hurts so much?" the woman asks angrily. "It should be him! It isn't fair that I have to suffer while he gets off completely free!"

Forgiveness Does Not Come Easily

You know what she needs. She needs to forgive. But you also know that when a person is terribly hurt by the sin of another, forgiveness does not come easily. The woman wants the one who caused the problem to "get what's coming to him." It is hard to be badly hurt this way and not want to get even. Forgiveness may be God's way, but it really doesn't seem fair!

Forgiveness *is* God's way, and it *is* fair. In fact, forgiveness is more for the benefit of the victim than it is for the offender. Anger and hatred and bitterness and resentment are destructive emotions. They tear out the very heart of our relationship with the Lord. To forgive, the victim has to give up those destructive emotions, including the desire to punish, the need to blame, and the feeling of superiority over that "greater sinner."

"I don't think I *can* forgive him," she tells you flatly.

You respond that no one expects forgiveness to come easily or quickly. That sometimes happens, but not usually. The deeper the wound, the longer and more difficult the process. We shouldn't expect it during the crisis stage. Only later, when the crisis is over, can the wronged person be guided to an attitude of Christian forgiveness.

Sometimes forgiveness will be granted sooner if the victim comes to understand what is going on inside the offender that contributed to his hurtful actions. This may mean persuading her to work with a counselor. Understanding, however, is not the same as excusing. With few exceptions, the offender had a choice. He didn't *have* to act the way he did.

"I just wish I could make him suffer like he has made me suffer!" the woman says bitterly.

You remind her that vengeance belongs to the Lord. If someone needs to be taught a lesson, God will do the teaching. If someone needs to be punished, God will do the punishing. Romans 12 is a good chapter for counselor and client to read together: "Do not take revenge, my friends, but leave room for God's wrath. . . . Do not be overcome by evil, but overcome evil with good" (vv. 19, 21 NIV).

Another action that will make it easier for her to forgive is to take a realistic look at herself. Without a doubt there are matters in her own life for which others have had to forgive her.

And how about the forgiveness of God? Even in the best and most righteous of us there is much that needs His forgiveness (Romans 3:22–23; 6:23). Christians who find it hard to forgive others will do well to reflect on the forgiveness they themselves have received from God (Ephesians 4:32).

"People have talked to me before about forgiveness," the woman says. " 'Forgive and forget' they tell me. Perhaps with God's help I will be able to forgive. But forget? Never!"

She may have a point. Is it really possible, even after forgiving another for the wrongs committed against you, to forget the whole thing? Well, yes and no. It is possible for God. Isaiah says, ". . . you have put all my sins behind your back" (Isaiah 38:17). God Himself promises, ". . . I will forgive their wickedness and will remember their sins no more" (Jeremiah 31:34). The psalmist tells us that "as far as the east is from the west, so far has he removed our transgressions from us" (Psalm 103:12, all NIV). When God forgives sins, they are gone. Not only does He not see them, but He doesn't even remember them!

But that's God. For us the past is not so easily erased. Wounds can heal, but the scars remain. Nor can all the consequences of what has happened be undone.

Don't tell the woman to look back at her painful experience as if it had never happened. She probably cannot do that. But though the memory isn't erased, the hatred, the malice, and the desire for revenge can be. She can't forget? That's all right. God asks her to forgive.

"I know you're right," she says thoughtfully. "I do need to forgive. But how do I do it?"

This is another important question. How do we set about forgiving a person who has caused us great injury? The answer is, we can't. Not in our own power. Forgiving great hurts and laying the past to rest are only possible through the power of God.

There is another side to forgiveness too. When a Christian is an alcoholic or an adulterer or an abuser of his wife or child, when he or she commits any blatant sin, the Christian community usually reacts with shock and shame and anger.

But what if that person repents and claims God's forgiveness? How does the Christian community respond to her then? Will the person who committed the sin be accused of getting off too easily? Or of not getting the punishment he deserves? Many Christians, feeling that they themselves have not sinned so greatly, find it difficult to accept such a person as their spiritual equal. The apostle Paul had some words for the church of Corinth on this subject: consider 2 Corinthians 2:5–11.

The Results of Suffering

The suffering a person endures can build trust and confidence in God, or it can destroy her faith. It can encourage a deeper fellowship in dependence on Him, or it can drive a wedge between herself and God. Problems can either make a person more sensitive to the suffering of others, or they can make her bitter or depressed. She can become more conscious of her need of God and more aware of His presence, or she can become angry and bitter toward Him. Perhaps one of the best things we as counselors can do is to lead a hurting person away from asking, "Why did this happen to me?" to asking, "Since this did happen to me, how am I going to respond to it?"

God gives us the capacity to respond to the ills and joys of life either constructively or destructively. Whatever our response, God's love remains constant. His presence is always there, whether or not we recognize or acknowledge it.

Does God want people to suffer? No, He does not. Nor does He necessarily send suffering for the purpose of bringing about some greater good. But people do suffer—good people, even Christians. This is a fact of life. Whether or not God causes the suffering, He can allow good to come from even the worst of events. He can and He does. Every one of us should be open to receive the growth and blessings He will bring to us through difficult circumstances.

You tell the woman that you can understand her asking, "Why?" You also tell her that you don't know the answer. You urge her to replace the "why" with "what will I do with what has happened to me?" If you can guide her to such a change of approach, to rest contentedly in the knowledge that her sovereign, loving God is in control, you have done your job well.

DOS AND DON'TS

Do ...

- Comfort the distressed woman with the truth that forgiving takes time.
- Encourage her to ask the Lord for help in handling her anger, her hatred, her desire for revenge, and any other destructive emotions she may harbor.
- Allow the person in pain to express her feelings freely, including negative emotions like anger and hatred.
- Emphasize that God really does forgive our past and our sins are removed from us "as far as the east is from the west."
- Remind her that although God never promised to keep us from problems and troubles, He did promise that we will never be separated from Him.
- Assure her that although she can grow and mature through this ordeal, it may take a long time to work through the problem.
- Urge her to use the experience to help and encourage other hurting people.
- Assure the person who has confessed her sins and has received forgiveness from God that her forgiveness does not depend on the approval of others.
- Stand with a woman who is struggling to set her life in order. Support and encourage her on her journey toward healing.
- Affirm God's power to heal and restore, however shattering an experience may be.
- Pray, pray, and pray some more. Pray with the victim and the offender. Pray *for* them too. Ask a few select, discreet friends also to uphold them in prayer. (You should do this without disclosing names or details.)

Don't ...

- Be guilty of offering superficial or simplistic answers to complex problems and questions. Don't respond with platitudes.
- Feel that you have to have an answer for every question. Sometimes the best response is an honest "I don't know."
- Suggest that God rescues people *because* they pray or trust in Him. Never even intimate that God didn't rescue this woman because she failed to pray or didn't trust Him enough.
- Scold or shame her for mourning too much or for not recovering as quickly as you think she should.
- Liken the suffering of your client at the hands of a violent person to Jesus on the cross. Don't suggest that she, like Jesus, should bear her cross without complaining.
- Encourage her to be "victorious" in the face of sorrow.
- Challenge her to be a "testimony" to others while she herself is still struggling to recover.

SUGGESTED READING

Allen, Blaine. *When God Says No.* Nashville: Thomas Nelson, 1981.

Augsburger, David. *The Freedom of Forgiveness.* Chicago: Moody, 1973.

Davis, Creath. *Lord, If I Ever Needed You, It's Now.* Palm Springs: Ronald N. Haynes, n.d.

Davis, Ron Lee. *A Forgiving God in an Unforgiving World.* Eugene, Ore.: Harvest House, 1985.

Donnelly, Doris. *Learning to Forgive.* Nashville: Abingdon, 1982.

Falwell, Jerry. *When It Hurts Too Much to Cry.* Wheaton, Ill.: Tyndale House, 1984.

Landorf, Joyce. *Irregular People.* Waco, Tex.: Word Books, 1982.

Lewis, C. S. *A Grief Observed.* London: Farber and Farber, 1966.

_____. *The Problem of Pain.* New York: Macmillan, 1962.

Lutzer, Erwin W. *When a Good Man Falls.* Wheaton, Ill.: Victor Books, 1985.

> A look at how a Christian can become effective again after falling into sin.

Martin, Grant. *Transformed by Thorns.* Wheaton, Ill.: Victor Books, 1985.

Merrill, Dean. *Another Chance.* Grand Rapids: Zondervan, 1981.

Murphree, Jon Tal. *A Loving God and a Suffering World.* Downers Grove, Ill.: InterVarsity, 1981.

Powell, Paul W. *Why Me, Lord?* Wheaton, Ill.: Victor Books, 1981.

Rice, John R. *When a Christian Sins.* Chicago: Moody, 1954.

Smedes, Lewis B. *Forgive and Forget.* San Francisco: Harper & Row, 1984.

Swindoll, Charles. *Improving Your Serve.* Waco, Tex.: Word Books, 1981.

Includes an excellent chapter on forgiveness.

————. *Recovery.* Waco, Tex.: Word Books, 1985.
Wiersbe, Warren. *Why Us? When Bad Things Happen to God's People.* Old Tappan, N.J.: Fleming H. Revell, 1983.
Woods, B. W. *Christians in Pain.* Grand Rapids: Baker, 1982.
Yancey, Phillip. *Where Is God When It Hurts?* Grand Rapids: Zondervan, 1977.

LOCAL REFERENCES

LOCAL SUPPORT GROUPS

A group of loving, concerned Christian women who will pray with, listen to, comfort and support the victims of tragedies or problems.

NAME:

Number:

Notes:

NAME:

Number:

Notes:

NAME:

Number:

Notes:

PHYSICIANS

Medical doctors who are sensitive to depression or other physical conditions related to stressful and critical conditions.

NAME:

Number:

Notes:

NAME:

Number:

Notes:

NAME:

Number:

Notes:

PSYCHIATRISTS, PSYCHOLOGISTS, TRAINED COUNSELORS

NAME:

Number:

Notes:

NAME:

Number:

Notes:

NAME:

Number:

Notes: